TRINITY AND

ᴏᴏᴏᴏᴏᴏᴏᴏᴏᴏ

HOLY, HOLY, HOLY

Holy, Holy, Holy:

Worshipping the Trinitarian God

CHRISTOPHER COCKSWORTH

Series Editor: Stephen Sykes

DARTON · LONGMAN + TODD

First published in 1997 by
Darton, Longman and Todd Ltd
1 Spencer Court
140–2 Wandsworth High Street
London SW18 4JJ

ISBN 0–232–52187–5

A catalogue record for this book is available from the British Library.

Unless otherwise stated, the Scripture quotations used are
from the New Revised Standard Version, copyright Oxford University
Press, 1995.

Phototypeset by Intype London Ltd
Printed and bound in Great Britain by
Redwood Books, Trowbridge

To Tim, Ash, Sam and Seb
and the child within.

CONTENTS

FOREWORD
ooooooooo

Trinity and Truth is a series of theological books written by
authors convinced that there is truth to be spoken about
God, and that such truth is best explored when we speak
about God as Father, Son and Holy Spirit.

Such a claim for truth has always been controversial. In
the fourth Gospel's account of his trial before Pilate, Jesus
said, 'All who are not deaf to truth listen to my voice.' Pilate's
famous reply, 'What is truth?' was neither jest nor invitation
to philosophical debate. It was an expression of impatient
dissent. He intended to be understood as the sole arbiter of
truth, because his was (he believed) the dominant ideology.
And to illustrate how feeble were the claims of the 'king of
the Jews', whose invisible 'kingdom' seemed to be on the
point of collapse, Pilate had Jesus flogged.

Pilate's question has a post-modern ring about it. The
truth for him was the extent to which he could impose
his power over Jesus, and everyone else within range of his
voice. But, said the writer of the fourth Gospel, this mockery
of a judicial process contained a reversal of appearances. It
is the judge who is judged. The prince of this world turns
out to be powerless. There is another truth, which is a way,
which leads to life.

In the long and turbulent history of Christian theology it
has often been forgotten that belief in the Trinity entails a
way of life. To many the doctrine of the Trinity has seemed
too erudite to be relevant; and in truth theologians have not

ix

always avoided a self-defeating level of detailed pseudo-precision. But the fearsome complexities of the classic disputes of the early centuries are not the main concern of this series. The authors intend, instead, to demonstrate trinitarian theology at work in the exploration and elucidation of modern questions.

Augustine of Hippo once pointed out that merely to utter the names, Father, Son and Holy Spirit, is physically to separate the sounds in time, and so to be misleading about the unity of 'substance' or 'being' of the three; for there is an irreplaceable history or narrative attaching to each of these names. And so what we signify when we utter the simple word 'God', is rich, complex and full of resource.

It is the purpose of this series to draw upon the continuing resourcefulness of trinitarian theology. The books will not be restricted to expositions of classic doctrines, but will concern every aspect of Christian life, worship and spirituality. Ancient orthodoxy was never intended to be a static, backward-looking set of intellectual constraints. It is the belief of the authors of this series that the trinitarian traditions of the Church are subversive and liberating convictions founded upon a willingness to listen freshly to the voice of truth.

STEPHEN SYKES
Bishop of Ely

PREFACE

ᴏᴏᴏᴏᴏᴏᴏᴏᴏᴏ

When I am with liturgists I want to talk about doctrine. When I am with systematic theologians I want to talk about worship. Sometimes it is difficult to get a sustained conversation going. But this is not so with the doctrine of the Trinity. Liturgists – and by that I mean anyone seriously interested in the service of God in worship – want to explore the implications of the trinitarian pattern of Christian worship. Systematic theologians recognize that without proper attention to the realities of worship, the origin and character of the doctrine cannot be appreciated and they are ready to discover more about its vitality in the worshipping life of the Church.

So for some time I have felt that a book was needed to draw together the interests and insights of both disciplines in the common quest for a deeper understanding of the trinitarian God and a fuller participation in God's life of love. And as someone who tries to keep a foot in both camps, I have wanted to have a go at such a book. I am grateful to all who have assisted me to do so, especially to David Pytches and Kenneth Stevenson for their consistent support, to David and Anne Sweeney and Andrew Facey for advice at an early stage of production, to Dan Hardy for encouragement at a late stage of production, to Alvyn Pettersen for helpful conversations in the middle stages, to Richard Bauckham for sending me a copy of his 1996 Didsbury Lectures, to Stephen Sykes for his guidance throughout the project,

Preface

to Matthew Morgan for work on the index and to Morag
Reeve and the rest of the DLT team for their kindness.
Without the help of all of these the faults and failings of the
book would have been greater. Those which remain, of
course, are my responsibility.

My deep gratitude also goes to my friend and former
colleague, Robert Hamilton, for four years of ministry
together in which we shared a love of the Trinity which I
shall treasure always. Finally, I want to acknowledge the
incalculable debt I owe to my wife Charlotte and to my
children for their patience and strength. Without my share
in the communion of their love it would have been much
harder for me to write about the share in the communion
of God's love which is extended to us in the activity of
worship.

INTRODUCTION
∞∞∞∞∞∞∞∞

1

ooooooooooo

The Trinity and Worship

If you are a theologian you will pray truly;
and if you pray truly you are a theologian.
(Evagrius of Pontus[1])

I A QUESTION OF IDENTITY

I switched on the radio and heard these words: 'You scratch anybody now and you will get people saying they believe in a god but it's a god of their own making'.[2] My mind immediately went back several centuries to the very different approach of St Francis of Assisi whose believing was based on these questions: 'Who are you, my dearest God? And what am I?'[3] Francis recognized that if our understanding of God is to be true to the way God is, then we have to listen to God speaking. Rather than define God in our way, we must allow God to define himself in his way. It is a matter of common sense and courtesy. In our ordinary dealings in life we can land ourselves in all sorts of trouble if we just form our own views about people without allowing them to describe themselves and explain what motivates and what concerns them. It is the same with God. It would be foolish and unfair to devise our own understanding of God and to refuse to engage with the way God has described himself.

Of course this sort of argument makes two large assumptions. The first is that God does speak. The second is that we

3

can hear what God says. Christian theology is based on the conviction that God does speak to his people. This book will accept that conviction. It will not attempt to justify it in any sort of philosophical way. But it will try to give this belief some content. Much of what follows will seek to explore how Christians believe God has spoken and to examine what God has said. Christian theology is also based on the belief that, despite all the fragility and fallibility of human thinking, it is still possible to conceive of God in ways that are true and faithful to the way God is – for God is able to work within and through the realities of our conceptual faculties, in order to enable us to receive that which he reveals. Again this book will accept that conviction. Although it will not attempt to provide a detailed philosophical defence of this position, it will seek to show by what means God does his work of allowing us to know and love him truly.

As I listened to the radio programme I discovered that it was part of a series examining the twentieth century. I joined it as the presenters were describing how they had been struck by the revival of religion in the latter part of the twentieth century. They knew that God had been declared 'dead' for over one hundred years. They had seen how serious thinkers in the 1930s held out very little hope for the future of religious belief. But in the 1990s they had observed an enormous interest in spirituality and religious faith. Nevertheless, they recognized that at least in the West this revival has little to do with institutional religion, which people generally either regard with suspicion or simply dismiss as irrelevant to their personal spiritual quest. They concluded that this increase in religious belief and activity is a form of 'individualized confessionalism' which has gone 'hand in hand with a dislocation and fragmentation of society'.[4] Others have noted how contemporary culture is marked by 'believing without belonging'.[5] People choose certain values and beliefs but they are content to live them out in apparent isolation from others who hold similar views.

St Francis' approach to truth and meaning was again very different. Rather than simply making up his own mind, from his own perspective, he believed that truth could only be known in relation to someone else, and ultimately only in relation to God. He had to ask a question and then listen to the answer. He remained free in all this. It was his question, he had to listen to the answer and then choose whether to receive it as God's truth but none the less he was not in it alone. The truth was to be discovered through contact and conversation. He knew that the truth could only be received in relation to the giver of truth.

There are two more things we need to note about Francis before we move on. The first is that his question came from faith by prayer. He calls God 'my dearest God'. He has already taken the step of believing in God and now seeks to know more of God. All our knowing is like this. We have to accept that something 'is' before we can begin our investigation. Even a highly theoretical scientific equation has to be considered as 'being' in some way before it can be tested. It is the same with God. We can only discover who God is if we allow ourselves to work within the assumption that God exists and that he wants us to know him. If the testing should prove the assumption false, so be it. But without the initial trusting, there can be no proper testing. Francis' question is also a prayer. Our thinking about God has to be rooted in prayer because this is the way we relate to God. Without some form of encounter in which we ask, listen and discern, our thinking about God will not get very far. Secondly, Francis does not think and pray alone. In one sense he does. In fact the incident took place when he was on retreat on Mount Verna. But in another sense he does not. Indeed we only hear about it because Brother Leo, who came to bring him provisions, overheard him. Leo was a member of the community Francis founded – a community within the community of the Church. Although intensely personal, his thoughts and prayers were themselves rooted in a community of faith and related to what others had thought about God and how others had prayed to God.

The role of prayer in the process of knowing the truth of God and the part the praying community plays in our grasp of this truth will be two of the main themes of this book. Before we begin to grapple with them we need to stay with the central Christian claim that God has spoken. God has spoken to reveal who he is. God has given his self-revelation. God has shown himself to be the trinitarian God of love. There was a time when theologians showed little interest in the doctrine of the Trinity. In recent years all this has changed. Theologians from across the nations and denominations seem to have discovered that the doctrine of the Trinity has been a sort of church Cinderella – something of great beauty and vitality, able to bring life and joy but which has been treated like an object of insignificance, embarrassment and sometimes even contempt. Actually the liturgy of the Church has never allowed it to be closeted away but has kept the doctrine in the prayers of the people if not in the studies of the theologians. Now thankfully, in many cases the two have come together and this series of books on *The Trinity and Truth* is just one example of this among many.[6]

This renaissance of trinitarian theology has a central emphasis. Three witnesses from different countries and traditions give its flavour. Walter Kasper, a German Roman Catholic, writes 'the trinitarian confession is . . .*the Christian form of speaking about God*'.[7] Thomas Torrance, a Scottish Reformed theologian, says that the doctrine of the Trinity is '*the distinctively Christian conception of God* with which every Christian doctrine and every aspect of the Christian way of life are concerned . . . the nerve and centre of them all'.[8]

Robert Jenson, a North American Lutheran, calls it the 'proper name for God' – the way God has named or revealed himself to be.[9] All three, together with many other voices, are making the point that the doctrine of the Trinity is not a remote, obscure piece of theoretical speculation with little relation to the Bible and to the ordinary details and demands of Christian living, but rather the self-description of the God of the Bible who is found in the ordinary details and demands of Christian life.

I used to drive past a church with a 'roadside pulpit' – a large poster board displaying a different caption or question each week designed to make the motorist think and question. Just before Christmas one year it said 'What do you most *need* for Christmas?' I noticed someone had scrawled their own answer at the bottom of the poster. It read 'Freedom from Monotheism'. I found this an interesting and ironic response because I had the feeling that the person who wrote it may have found what he or she was looking for in the very claims of Christmas itself. It may be pure speculation but I had a hunch that this writer of clever graffito was dissatisfied with notions of a distant deity, existing in splendid isolation and untouched by the affairs of the world. Christmas also rejects such notions. It claims that God exists as an eternal round of love and that his nature of giving and receiving propels him first to create a world to share in his love and then to enter that world as the beloved through the power of the lover's love, to defeat all that holds the world back from an ever deeper enjoyment of his love. To be sure this is not an abandonment of monotheism but it is, as Kasper says, 'the Christian form of monotheism',[10] which as Torrance says 'actually conflicts sharply with generally accepted beliefs and established ideas in human culture and initiates a seismic reconstruction not only of religious and intellectual belief but of the foundations of human life and knowledge'.[11]

II THE LENS OF WORSHIP

Our task in this book is to look at the Trinity through the lens of worship. This is not simply a very helpful and accessible way of approaching the Trinity but also a very proper way – perhaps *the* proper way.[12] Here are three reasons why the perspective of worship is such an appropriate one to consider the Christian claim that the one God exists eternally as the Trinity of Father, Son and Holy Spirit.

The first is that we encounter the Trinity in worship. This is true in the sense that Christian worship has a necessarily trinitarian structure. In order to be *Christian* worship it must refer in some way to Jesus as well as to God and in so doing it will inevitably refer to Jesus' Spirit at work amongst his people. As a teenager I was involved in a Christian youth movement. I have no recollection of anyone talking directly about the doctrine of the Trinity but I do remember times of worship in which we sang songs to God about Jesus, sometimes singing to Jesus himself, knowing that we did so because God's Spirit was lifting our hearts to give thanks for the gift of his Son. I know that from an early point I learnt to form my prayers in a trinitarian sort of way. I always ended my prayers by saying 'in Jesus' name' and I felt that my prayers were in some way guided, or at least motivated, by God's Spirit. At the same time I used to attend a Baptist church at which I was often struck by the minister's ability to pray very full and rich extemporary prayers. They were trinitarian. They gave thanks for all that God had done through Christ and they prayed for the work of God's Spirit as we gathered to sing God's praises and hear God's word. Later I started going to Evensong in the parish church where recently I had been confirmed. One refrain resounded again and again around that large thirteenth-century building: 'Glory be to the Father and to the Son and to the Holy Ghost'. This was the name into which I had been baptized as a child in that same church many years before. In the early days of my life, well before I was able to comprehend anything of its meaning, I was introduced to the Trinity in the worship of the Church.

Our encounter with the Trinity in worship goes beyond the empirical fact that when we take part in Christian worship we sing hymns, say prayers and receive blessings which have a trinitarian character. Participation in worship can penetrate to the deeper levels of our experience and become a genuine engagement with God. At times like this we feel the touch of God's Spirit. We know, even if just for a moment, that God has come so close that we can almost feel his breath. We know that what is going on within us is our own and yet it is more than us. There is something welling up which we have not caused. It is joy and peace and gratitude together with a deep sense of well-being. We feel we can hardly hold it within us. We must speak or sing it out. God's goodness is almost palpable. It creates within us a rush of love for God. We know that such goodness and such love cannot be separated from Jesus Christ. Perhaps we have been moved by exquisite sounds of music, by a powerful sermon, by receiving communion or simply by the silence of being in God's presence. The content of each will in some way have been filled with the fullness of Christ. The goodness of God which has been mediated to us by word or sacrament, music or silence, will have had to do with Christ. The love which we feel for God will be expressed with reference to Christ. The praise or prayer which we offer to God will be because of God's goodness we see in Jesus. We know that it is through Christ that God has reached us and through Christ that we reach God.

Now I am not suggesting that we have this level of experience every time we worship. Sometimes we will be much lower down the scale. The point I want to make is that even in those less heady moments, our engagement with God in

9

worship is more than a unitarian experience. It has a Christ and Spirit dimension. It is a differentiated experience. It is trinitarian. If you resonate with this even in the faintest sort of way, that is, if you find yourself, when you pray and worship, doing so with reference to Jesus and his Spirit, then you have the basic structures in place which this book is simply trying to identify, clarify and edify.

In the fourth century Evagrius of Pontus said that: 'If you are a theologian you will pray truly; and if you pray truly you are a theologian'.[13] He meant that if our talk *about* God is correct our talk *to* God will be right and likewise, if our talk *to* God is correct our talk *about* God will be right. Both will be correct if they are faithful to the way God has shown himself to be. Because God has addressed us as the one God who is Father, Son and Holy Spirit we are to address him in the same way.

It may be that all kinds of language issues come to mind at this point, such as, 'Do I have to use these exact words, which for all sorts of reasons I find somewhat alienating, to pray truly?' I want to defer these sorts of questions until later in this chapter because, although important, they do not bear directly on the critical point at issue. The point is that if our worship of God is related to Christ and to the Spirit, then we can call ourselves trinitarian theologians because we are faithfully engaging with the true reality of God. Trinitarian theology is not a kind of higher mathematics for the theologically initiated. In fact it is more like the lowest common denominator for the believers. It is simply talking about the God to whom we speak when we pray in the name of Jesus and by the power of the Spirit.

Another reason for looking at the Trinity from the perspective of worship is because of the liturgical origins of the doctrine. In Part One of the book we will be doing the hard work of examining the faith first of the New Testament writers and churches and then of those who followed them in the next few centuries. Two things should become clear. The first is that Christian worship assumed a distinctly trinitarian character from the earliest stage. It was as the early Christians worshipped God that the trinitarian pattern of their experience of salvation came into sharpest focus. The second is that the phenomenon of worship played a critical role in the process of understanding this experience and working through all its implications which finally led to the credal statements of the fourth century when the doctrine of the Trinity was formally and officially stated. Worship served as a criterion of orthodoxy. It did so in two ways. First it preserved worship for God alone. Only God could be worshipped. The worship of anything or anyone else was not only unorthodox, it was blasphemous. Second, it protected the authentic worshipping life of the Church. The Church's experience of God in worship was a true experience of God, therefore the implications of that worship had to be followed through into the Church's understanding of God. The explicit formulation of the doctrine of the Trinity was the result of holding these two concerns together. Crudely speaking, the role of Jesus and the Spirit in the worshipping life of the Church led to a new way of conceiving the one God, a way which included them in the one reality of God.

A third reason for looking at the Trinity through worship is because of the interconnection between worship and theology, or more strictly between doxology and theology. Theology simply means thought, word, speech (*logos*) about God (*Theos*). Doxology means thought, word, speech (*logos*) about glory (*doxa*). Theological statements are words about God. Because God is the one to whom glory (honour, dignity, value) ultimately belongs, theological statements are doxological statements. Every statement about God, if it is true to the way God is, is an acknowledgement of God's glory, an affirmation of his true divinity. It is an expression

11

of praise. Jürgen Moltmann says that 'Real theology, which means the knowledge of God, finds expression in thanks, praise and adoration. And it is what finds expression in doxology that is real theology'. The doctrine of the Trinity qualifies as 'real theology' because it is about knowing God and its proper place is not in the textbooks of the scholars but on the lips of the worshippers. This is not to disparage the work of theologians, it is just to affirm that the function of any theological study of the Trinity is to lead us into a deeper participation in the worship of the Triune God. Augustine would have agreed. He ended his great tome on the Trinity not with an argument but with a prayer.[14] In Part Two we will be exploring the Trinity with the help of three doxological concepts or categories – the glory of God, the invitation of Christ and the searching of the Spirit. Because they arise from the world of worship, these categories are particularly suitable for the task.

We need to spend some more time on the relationship between theology and worship to explore it more fully. There is a close connection between our salvation and worship. The God who saves is the God we worship. We can see this clearly in the account of Israel's liberation from Egypt: Moses was told by the Lord to 'Go to Pharaoh and say to him, "Thus says the Lord: let my people go, so that they may worship me"' (Exod. 8:1). God wanted his people to be released from their burden of oppression and captivity so that they could worship in freedom. And that is what happened. The first thing the people of Israel did when they found themselves safe on the other side of the Red Sea was to sing:

> The LORD [YHWH] is my strength and my might,
> and he has become my salvation;
> this is my God, and I will praise him,
> my father's God, and I will exalt him.

12

The LORD [YHWH] is a warrior;
The LORD [YHWH] is his name. (Exod.15:2–3)

They worshipped God. Their salvation found instinctive expression in worship. The content of their worship reflected the characteristics of their salvation and the character of the Saviour. A small, insignificant group of people, trapped in a violent and ruthless form of exploitation, had been set free from the power of a mighty empire. The waters of the sea had parted to give them safe passage. The same waters had overpowered the advancing Egyptian troops with their chariots and horses. They were bursting with praise. They worshipped God as the strong redeemer, the warrior who had liberated them. The song goes on to affirm YHWH's lordship over nature and over all the nations and concludes by rejoicing that 'YHWH will reign for ever and ever' (15:18).

Zechariah, father of John the Baptist, also makes the connection between salvation and worship in his prophetic song of praise:

> This was the oath he swore to our father Abraham:
> to set us free from the hands of our enemies,
> Free to worship him without fear,
> holy and righteous in his sight,
> all the days of our life. (Luke 1:73–5)

Here freedom to worship is seen as the essence of the salvation which God had promised to his people. Zechariah prophesies that the time for the complete fulfilment of the promise had dawned. Because the coming salvation was already breaking into the world, the promised praise was also already breaking out on his lips as it had on Mary's and soon would on Simeon's.

As we shall see in chapter 3, Luke carefully ends his Gospel where he began – with a scene of worship. He tells us that as soon as Jesus ascended to heaven, the disciples worshipped him. The saving events of Jesus' death, resurrection and ascension compelled one response – worship. Now, however, Jesus is included in the worship which belongs to the one God. Luke is telling us that Jesus was so intimately associated with the action of salvation that he could not be disassociated from the response to salvation. As with the liberation from Egypt in the old covenant, so with the liberation from sin and death in the new, we see the character of the salvation being reflected back in the content of the worship and through this we begin to discern the identity of the God who saves.

Worship is like the great cheer echoing around a football stadium as the critical goal is scored and victory is secured. Like the roar of the crowd, worship tells us that something has happened which has made a difference to the way things are. And as we listen to the chant, we can tell who scored the goal.

There is also a close connection between revelation and worship. Revelation involves reception. It is all too easy to think of revelation as some sort of divine TV show beamed to the writers of the Bible who were mere spectators, lazing back in their armchairs, required only to press the record button on the video recorder so that it could be played back before our eyes as a ready-made piece of canned information. In fact, the process of revelation is much closer to the art of good journalism and responsible reading. Just as the journalist has to use the skills of research, analysis and interpretation, so the biblical writers played their critical role in discerning and understanding the work of God's revelation. And just as we have to assess and weigh what we read in the papers before we accept it as fair and accurate, so we play our part in reflecting on the revelation before we receive it as God's truth and allow it to change our lives. The Swiss theologian, Karl Barth, was insistent on our dependence upon God's revelation and our inability to know the truth of God by ourselves, but he nevertheless recognized that the process of revelation involves God making us capable of receiving his truth. Barth said that this is how God completes his revelation.

The worship of the early Christians was a primary environment in which God opened the hearts and eyes of his people to see his revelation. This is evident in the Emmaus story in Luke's Gospel – a story redolent with the continuing experience of the risen Christ in the worship of the early Christian communities. As the word is unfolded the people's 'hearts burn within them' (24:32). They begin to grasp the pattern and purpose of God in the suffering of Christ. As the bread is broken the people's 'eyes are opened' (24:31). They recognize that Jesus is among them. They rejoice that Christ is truly risen and and active in their midst.

In John's Gospel Jesus told the Samaritan woman that there would come a time when people would worship 'the Father in spirit and truth' (4:23). Before his death he promised that the Spirit would come to them to lead them into truth (16:13). Gregory of Nazianzus, a fourth-century Christian leader who played a significant role in the formulation of the doctrine of the Trinity, claimed that the Spirit was 'resident and active' in the Church, first revealing the divinity of the Father, then showing the divinity of the Son and finally demonstrating his own divinity. Through the Spirit's inspiration of the worship of the Church in the early centuries of its life, God's people were able to discern in depth who God had declared himself to be in Christ, so as, in Barth's words, 'to complete his revelation'.[15]

The same work of the Spirit goes on amongst us as we worship. Worship continues to be a revelatory event, not in the sense of adding anything to what God has said of himself in Christ as attested in the Scriptures, for God has spoken his final word in Christ, but in the sense of taking us into a

15

fuller understanding of this final word and leading us into a more faithful following of that word in all the particularities of our lives today. In worship we spend time with God. We attend to the ways by which the Church has always been built. We engage with the apostles' teaching. We take part in the breaking of bread. We join in the prayers. We play our part in the fellowship. In all these ways God takes us deeper into his truth. He shows us that he is *for us*. He reveals that he has bound himself in covenant to us and that he has drawn us into the presence of his Son by the power of his Spirit. As we worship, God crafts the contours of his life into our lives so that his trinitarian being becomes not an impossible thing to believe before breakfast in Alice of Wonderland fashion, but a reality known in our depths because it is a love which has caught us and captivated us and made us cry:

> Batter my heart, three person'd God; for you
> As yet but knocke, breathe, shine, and seek to mend;
> That I may rise, and stand, o'erthrow mee, 'and bend
> Your force, to breake, blowe, burn and make me new.

* * *

> Take mee to you, imprison mee, for I
> Except you'enthrall mee, never shall be free,
> Nor ever chast, except you ravish mee.[16]

III AN ISSUE OF LANGUAGE

Christian worship traditionally addresses 'the three person'd God' as Father, Son and Holy Spirit. There can be no doubt that many find this particular name a difficult one to utter in their worship, not because they are disillusioned with the concept of the trinitarian God but because they find the language of God as Father, and in some cases, the language of God as Son, extremely alienating. Anyone

16

involved in pastoral ministry will know of the many who have been deeply and deliberately damaged by dysfunctional father figures. They have been the victims of serious abuse and are still suffering its effects, so much so that they find it desperately difficult to identify God with fatherhood, especially in their worship. Others may have been less explicitly abused but still find it difficult to relate to God as Father. Perhaps this is because of some sort of disruption or breakdown of their relationship with their own father caused not by deliberate abuse but through the ordinary failures of human relationships. Or it may be because notions of God's fatherhood carry unavoidable connotations of certain forms of male behaviour which they have found highly unattractive or even exploitative.

All of these difficulties can be found in men as well as women but there are particular problems which many women find themselves facing when asked to relate to God using language which has a literal association with men rather than women. Because fatherhood and sonship are by definition beyond their experience as women (in that they cannot be fathers and sons), many women have claimed that they are required to make a much greater leap of imagination than men when it comes to relating to God through the language of fatherhood and sonship. All men know what it is to be a son and many have direct experience of being a father. There is a natural connection between their experience of being human and the language we use about God. Women's experience as daughters and mothers, on the other hand, seems to have no basis in the identity of God and therefore, so the argument goes, the traditional language will always be alienating – sometimes on a very conscious level, at others on a more subconscious level, but always presenting a problem to be overcome.

These are real issues in our contemporary culture. They are not just to do with changes in attitudes to language which have undermined the traditional convention in the English language of using masculine words and images in an inclusive way so as to refer to women as well as men. The issues are driven by the changing role of women in contemporary society, leading to huge shifts in women's understanding of themselves and perception of everything, and by genuine gospel concerns such as justice, liberation, truth and the promise of reconciliation with God for all people, regardless of wealth, race or gender.

Some feminist theologians have decided that the problems are insoluble. They have concluded that Christianity is simply incompatible with the religious needs and aspirations of women. They have given up on Christian faith in search of a post-Christian God. Others have embarked on a strategy either to replace traditional language about God with another more accessible and acceptable version or to place these other forms of language alongside the traditional formula as equal alternatives. This strategy is based on the claim that our language about God is metaphorical. We take images from our own experience and apply them to God while at the same time knowing that these are only pictures or parables which help us conceive of God. They are not literal statements about him. We say that God is a rock, a fortress or a warrior whilst at the same time knowing that God is not literally any of these. The same applies when we call God 'Father'. We are taking an image from our own experience and applying it to God, believing that is a helpful way of depicting God which illustrates something about the character of God. For those for whom it is an unhelpful way of depicting God, bringing to their minds all sorts of associations which are far removed from the character of God, other more helpful metaphors should be used.[17]

However, there is another way of understanding the language we use about God. Rather than seeing our language as ways by which we choose to make sense of God, we can see it as God's gift to us through which God communicates the way he is. This means that we must relate the language first to God's self-depiction, that is to God's use of the language, rather than to our own use of the language in the normal course of our human experience. Our language describes what we see and is therefore limited to what is revealed by the particular object to which it refers. God's revelation of himself to us demands a reconstruction of our language so it can properly and faithfully refer to him.

We can see this sort of process taking place with the use of the word 'Father' in relation to God. There is a noticeable reticence to name God 'Father' in the Old Testament. In fact God is only called Father eleven times and is not once addressed in prayer as 'Father'.[18] Hebrew religion radically distinguished God from the divine procreators of Canaanite religion. YHWH, the Lord, was the creator of sexuality. He did not create through the passion of his own sexuality – either male or female – but through the freedom of his compassionate love. YHWH is not a male or female deity in need of a consort. He is the sovereign Lord, complete in himself, who creates all human beings, male and female, in his image. The people of Israel are God's people not because they have been biologically generated, but because they have been graciously adopted by God. Once freed from associations of male sexuality, the title of Father came to be used by psalmists and prophets as a way of depicting YHWH's relationship of liberating love with his people. YHWH is the Father of Israel because he has bound himself in a covenant of love with them.

In Christ we find the covenant relationship concentrated and fulfilled. Jesus lives out the faithful covenant love which YHWH looks for in Israel and experiences the covenanted closeness of God to his people. Jesus knows himself to be the Son of the Father. As we shall see in chapter 2, he dares to call God *Abba*, an address of astounding intimacy taken

19

from the family relations of his time. He describes God as Father in his teaching but in a way which smashes the contemporary stereotypes of fatherhood in his culture. Only the father who waits day after day watching the distant horizon for his rebellious son and who then, contrary to all convention, hitches up his clothes, runs to greet his returning son and then throws himself upon him in unimaginably affectionate generosity – only this sort of father can begin to give us a glimpse of the God Jesus knows as Father. As well as describing God as Father in his teaching, Jesus prays to God as Father and, moreover, gives the gift of sharing in his relation of love with him to those who ask to pray as he prays. He teaches them to say 'Our Father'.

The concept of God as Father which we see emerging in the later prophets becomes a lived reality in the life of Jesus and in the people who respond to his invitation to live his way and to speak his words. To speak to God as Father will never be easy. We have all suffered at the hands of father figures, though some much more than others. We have all been victims of the abuse of male power, though some more than others. But as the French philosopher Paul Ricoeur has said,

> Far, therefore, from the addressing of God as father being easy, along the lines of a relapse into archaism, it is rare, difficult, and audacious, because it is prophetic, directed toward fulfilment rather than toward origins. It does not look backward toward a great ancestor, but forward, in the direction of a new intimacy on the model of the knowledge of the son.[19]

If we find 'Father' a difficult way of addressing God we cannot simply replace it with 'Mother'. To do so would be to say that the Fatherhood of God referred to gender rather than grace. Neither can we replace it with 'Creator', or some other word describing God's action. To do so would fail to recognize that God is only God the Creator in relation to his action of creating the world. God is God the Father in relation to his own being as God because he is eternally in a relation of love with God the Son. God has been the Creator since the beginning of time, but the Father from all eternity.

To be faithful to the witness of Jesus, we must grapple with the God he reveals. This means refusing to project our damaged images and experiences of fatherhood and masculinity onto God but to allow him to reconstruct our image of his Fatherhood by the perfected experience of Jesus and the work of his Spirit in our midst. In this way, although 'the Fatherhood of God' may remain a metaphor, it none the less refers to what is real in a unique and irreplaceable way. This self-definition by God of what it means for him to be Father of the Son is powerfully depicted in a sixteenth-century painting by Baldung.[20] Christ has been taken from his cross and is being mourned by Mary and John. In the background is God the Father, his head to the side, grieving the death of his Son. His deity is shown in his bond of love with his Son. His power is shown in his willingness to suffer the loss of his Son. His majesty is shown in his strength to let nothing, neither death nor life, separate us from the love he has revealed in the giving of his Son.

Although 'Father' is a non-negotiable form of address to God (we cannot abandon it) and a normative form of address (it establishes a truth about God to which we are bound), it is by no means the only way of addressing God. The Bible and the worshipping tradition of the Church are full of a whole range of titles which help to focus one aspect of God's nature and then another. Part of the appeal of Celtic style worship to which many are attracted today, is the way it makes such good use of this rich quarry of words for God in its worship. By inspiring the imagination with all manner of very concrete images it seems able to lead people into a deeper understanding of God's nature, often providing a new appreciation of God's trinitarian life. It is worth remembering that the book of Revelation, which shows more interest in the Trinity and worship than any other book in the Bible, has a number of ways of describing the Trinity, none of them using anything near the traditional formula. One of the great strengths of some feminist writing on the Trinity is its ability to recover the different ways of naming the Trinity which can be found in the tradition of the Church and to experiment with new ones. The problems come when any of these confuse our calling to share in the relationship of love with the God and Father of our Lord Jesus Christ to which we are invited by the gospel.

This invitation is pictured in Andrei Rublev's fifteenth-century icon of the Holy Trinity which, like the doctrine of the Holy Trinity, has become enormously popular across the nations and denominations. It shows three figures around a table. There is a gentleness, calm and tenderness between them but also a great strength coming from their unity of love and purpose. The scene is holy, glorious and heavenly. It transcends the earth. Yet at the centre of the table stands a chalice filled with grapes and, behind the shoulder of one of the figures, a tree. These are signs of sacrifice and life. The way the transcendence is exercised is through self-giving for the saving of others. Despite all the heavenly glory an ordinary home can be seen in the background of the icon. The glory is manifested on earth. At the side of the table our side, the side we face is an open place, a space for us to eat and drink. The scene is an invitation. It calls us to step into the movement of adoration between the three figures. It beckons us to share in the worship of the trinitarian God.

PART ONE

ORIGINS
ᐤᐤᐤᐤᐤᐤᐤᐤᐤᐤ

2

The Shape of Worship in the New Testament

*So Christ came and proclaimed peace to you who were far off
and peace to those who were near, for through him
we both have access in the one Spirit to the Father.*
                                        (Ephesians 2:17–18)

I INTRODUCTION

There was a house in Corinth, next door to the synagogue.
It belonged to Titius Justus, a Roman with a liking for Jewish
religion. One room was overflowing with people. They were
a rare mix. Some were from the educated classes and
were clearly quite wealthy. Others, probably the majority,
were much lower down the Corinthian social strata. Some
were Jews, including a number of prominent members of
the Jewish community such as Crispus, the president of the
synagogue. Others were Greeks or Romans. A few were
from some of the other national communities found in
cosmopolitan Corinth. There were men and women and
even some children. It was a strange gathering. It was clearly
a religious meeting of some sort but there was neither the
order of the Jewish synagogue nor the rather hedonistic
ceremonies of the Greek temples. But there was a scroll in
the middle of the room – perhaps Crispus had brought it
from the synagogue – and there was a lot of noise as people
prayed and sang. One of the worshippers was a tent-maker
called Paul. He seemed to be the leader of the group. He

began speaking to them. He talked about the God of Israel and a person called Jesus. There was a tremendous sense of energy in the room which seemed to bind the people together in a common cause and an electrifying intensity of feeling in whatever was done.[1]

Who were these people? What were they doing? What did their alternative religion have to do with the traditions of Israel? Why was Jesus so important to them? What did they mean when they talked about the energy and power of the Spirit? These are the sort of questions we will be pursuing in this chapter and the next as we explore the origins of the understanding of God as Trinity. But before we do so it is worth making three general comments about how the biblical material needs to be handled.

First, we should avoid reading the New Testament through the eyes of later trinitarian orthodoxy.[2] This is not easy. Most of us have been formed by the Creeds or at least credal confessions – and that is no bad thing. It shows that the Creeds are doing their job of initiating us into the confession of the Church. In another way, however, we will miss the dynamic of the early Christian experience of God if we read the Scriptures assuming that all the writers of the New Testament had already *arrived* at a fully fledged trinitarian faith. The dynamic is the force of the impact of the event of Jesus Christ on the lives of those people, many of them Jewish, whom we call the first Christians. Our task, in this and in the next chapter, is to investigate the power of this force and the pattern it produced in the prayer and worship of the first Christian communities. We will discover a great deal of raw, rudimentary or primal trinitarianism in the experience of the early Christians but it is exactly its primal, almost eruptive character – rather like a volcano bursting with energy and blasting out of the existing structure – which makes it so alive and interesting. We do it a disservice if we treat it as a formal and fixed doctrine and so

26

turn the volcanic drama into a settled mountain scene in which the landscape is fully formed and everything already in its place.

The second comment is similar. There are a number of dangers into which we can unwittingly run when examining the pattern of worship in the New Testament.[3] It is easy to read back later practices into the worship of the New Testament period, assuming that because something happened in the third century it is being alluded to in a particular biblical text. It is also tempting, particularly for those with liturgical interests, to find echoes of a fixed form of Christian liturgy at almost every point in the New Testament writings. Again it is quite natural, but not necessarily correct, to assume that because a particular feature of worship is referred to in one part of the New Testament, it was common to all the Christian communities of the first century. All of these tendencies can also dissolve the dynamic of early Christian experience, seeing it as settled, fixed and uniform rather than fluid, developing and multiform. New Testament scholars currently call for sensitivity to the particular styles and interests of the different biblical writers and also to the diversity of the different Christian communities. Our task is to see how different writers, and correspondingly the different communities to which they were writing, articulated their experience of the events surrounding the person of Jesus to the God whom they believed had met and saved them in him. We are looking at how their experience of salvation was 'played back' as they responded to God in worship. John Calvin said that 'our faith has no true evidence, except that we call upon God'.[4] By examining how the different writers of the New Testament called upon God, I hope that the evidence of the early Christian encounter with him will become clearer.

The third general comment is that when analysing the biblical material our aim is not to try to seek out particular texts which will somehow prove that the doctrine of the Trinity is biblical. It is to discover the God of whom the Bible speaks and so discern the identity of the one who encounters us through Scripture.[5] The primary question is, 'Who is the God by whom the early Christian communities believed themselves to have been addressed and who goes on addressing us through their testimony?' As we said in the last chapter, the advantage of using worship as a tool with which to examine, or a window through which to view the early Christian experience of God, is that in worship the God who speaks is spoken to in return. And, in Robert Jenson's words, 'it is in liturgy when we do not talk about God but to and for him that we need to use his name, and that is where trinitarian formulas appear, both initially and to this day'.[6]

II SALVATION IN CHRIST AND THE BEGINNINGS OF TRINITARIAN PRAYER: ROMANS 8

Romans 8 may at first sight seem to be a strange place to begin exploring early Christian worship. Unlike in 1 Corinthians 11–14 Paul is not addressing specifically liturgical issues. Unlike the author of Acts he is not describing liturgical settings. Unlike the writer to the Hebrews he is not deliberately adopting a liturgical perspective. But first sights can be deceptive. Here in Romans 8 Paul is explaining to his hearers how they have been made Christians, how they can continue as Christians and how God will fulfil their Christian identity in the destiny that awaits them. Although the chapter is not directly about worship it is about how Christians are related to God and therefore intimately concerns how they relate to God in prayer and worship.

Paul has already handled the deep and demanding themes of sin and judgement, righteousness and faith, law and grace. On the basis of all this he can declare:

> There is therefore now no condemnation for those who are
> in Christ Jesus. For the law of the Spirit of life in Christ Jesus
> has set you free from the law of sin and death. For God has
> done what the law, weakened by the flesh, could not do: by
> sending his own Son in the likeness of sinful flesh, and to
> deal with sin, he condemned sin in the flesh, so that the just
> requirements of the law might be fulfilled in us, who walk
> not according to the flesh but according to the Spirit. (vv.
> 1–4)

This is the work of God. By sending his Son, God has
enabled the law, that is all his intentions for good in our
creation, to be fulfilled. Negatively this means that in the
judgement of the law, the condemnation of sin which God's
holy love demands has been made. The condemnation has
fallen not on sin in an abstract and detached way but in a
concrete and embodied way on that which brings sin about
– the sinner, sinful humanity, the flesh. And it has happened
as Christ has entered into the existence and conditions of
sinful humanity to stand in free but full solidarity with sinful
people to bear the judgement that is upon them. Positively,
it means that the best life which God's love expects, that is
the righteous, obedient life, has been formed in Christ and
is being forged in his people as they live according to the
Spirit.

When Paul says 'now', he is referring to the new eschatological time which has begun in Christ.[7] Eschatology means
word or speech (*logos*) about the end (*eschaton*). For Paul
and the witness of the New Testament generally, the end
time, the time of the fulfilment of God's promises had
happened in Christ. In the raising of Jesus from the dead
the first fruit of the resurrection of all has already appeared.
In the coming of the Spirit from the risen Christ the down
payment and guarantee of the eschatological life has been
given. In the glory of Jesus' ascension the glorification of

humanity within the glory of God and amongst the glory of the new creation has been inaugurated. As Paul said to the Corinthian church, to be in Christ is to be 'a new creation' (2 Cor. 5:17). It is to participate in the life of the new person: the one who, having accepted the condemnation of the old humanity in its sin and experienced its death, was raised into the justified or righteous life of the new humanity, which lives not according to the flesh (the way of fallen humanity) but according to the Spirit (the way of the new humanity).

Paul's personal experience of Christian life as well as his knowledge of the besetting problems of the various Christian communities with which he had dealings had given him ample evidence that although Christ's followers have been initiated into the eschatological life, its full form had still to be worked out in them. Paul defines this full form of salvation as the glory which God will reveal in them when he raises their 'mortal bodies' (v. 11) and conforms them 'into the image of his Son' (v. 29). Until that happens Christians face the constant danger of falling back into the world of the flesh, giving way to the sinful tendency of the old nature, rather than living out their new identity in the world of the Spirit. So Paul exhorts his readers, saying:

> For all who are led by the Spirit are children of God. For you did not receive a spirit of slavery to fall back into fear, but you received a spirit of adoption. When we cry, 'Abba! Father!' it is that very Spirit bearing witness with our spirit that we are children of God, and if children, then heirs, heirs of God and joint heirs with Christ – if, in fact, we suffer with him so that we may also be glorified with him. (vv. 14–17)

Here we come to the heart of the matter. Paul is at a critical point in his argument. His letter has demonstrated that righteousness has been established in Christ through his life obediently given up to death and through his resurrection

30

into the eschatological life. It has shown that the righteous life of Christ is available for the whole of humanity to share in by faith and baptism. But all this is threatened by the continual undercurrent drawing the people of God back into the old ways of the flesh which not only lead them away from the new life but undermine the very claim that God's eschatological promises have been fulfilled in Christ. Faced with this dilemma and tension of Christian existence, Paul directs the Roman Christians to the fundamental datum of their experience which lies at the heart of their personal prayer and at the heights of their corporate worship: 'When we cry "Abba! Father!" it is that very Spirit bearing witness with our spirit that we are children of God'.

In Karl Barth's commentary on the letter to the Romans – an exposition which changed the course of European theology in this century – there is an unsurpassed comment on these verses:

> We – God's children! Consider and bear in mind the vast unobservability, impossibility, and paradox of these words. Remember that, in daring this prediction, we are taking the miraculous, primal, creative step which Abraham took; we are taking the step of faith, the step over the abyss from the old to the new creation, which God alone can take. We – God's children! In uttering these words either we are talking blasphemy or we are singing the song of the redeemed. Whether it be on our lips the one or the other, we have dared to say it, when we have uttered the cry, *Abba, Father.* We never know or shall know or have known what it means, for we have done what no mortal man can or ought to do: we have made use of human words, 'as though' we had seen what no eye hath seen, 'as though' we had heard what had entered into no human ear, 'as though' there had come into our heart what no heart has contained. And yet, we cannot deny what we have said; for we have encountered height in the depth,

righteousness in sin, life in death, Christ in us. Hath God prepared this for them that love him?! Who dares to range himself amongst those that love God, for whom this hath been prepared? Yes, but who dares to exclude himself from their number? We have already included ourselves: we have uttered the word.[8]

Paul and the Roman Christians had uttered the word. By faith they had dared to call God '*Abba*, Father'. They knew they could not do so by themselves but only as enabled by the Spirit of the one who before them had spoken to God in this new and free way. This had become indeed 'the song of the redeemed' for as Luther said, 'faith expands the heart, the emotions and the voice',[9] and, as Calvin said, 'the spirit of adoption exhilarates our souls by bearing a testimony to our salvation'.[10] As Paul calls to the mind of his readers the raw material of their encounter with God, he has to use a trinitarian pattern. God had encountered them in such a way that although he could be distinguished from Christ and the Spirit, he could not be separated from them.

I remember a time during my training for ordination when each member of my tutor group was asked to give a one sentence definition of worship. At that time I was working for a research degree in the area of Christian worship so I gave what I thought was a suitably sophisticated answer. It was something on the lines of the offering of the whole of our lives to God in grateful self-giving. But, along with others in the group, I was much more moved by the answer of a young Church of Scotland ordinand on an exchange visit to the college. 'For me', he said, 'worship is joining with Jesus as he praises his Father.' He made the reality of Christian existence and the nature of Christian prayer and worship startlingly clear and simple. To be a Christian is to be in Christ through his Spirit. To relate to

God in prayer and worship is to do so *in, through* and even *with* Christ, 'the first born of many brothers' (8:29).

This is what Paul meant when he said that by the Spirit of adoption we cry *Abba!* Father! *Abba* is an Aramaic word which has no direct equivalent in English. Combining intimacy with respect, it was the word children used when speaking to their fathers. It was also the word Jesus used to talk to God. In a famous study of the words of Jesus, Joachim Jeremias claimed that not only was it beyond historical dispute that Jesus addressed God in this way but that his use of *Abba* was unprecedented in his time, and therefore shows that Jesus understood himself to be in a filial relationship with God of unique intimacy and intensity.[11] Since then pages of theological study have been devoted to examining Jeremias' claims and although his conclusions have been at times challenged and at points qualified, their substance has remained intact. For example, at the end of a careful study of sayings related to Jesus' sonship and a comparison with contemporaneous Jewish spirituality, James Dunn judged that:

> We are able to say, again with confidence, that Jesus understood and expressed his relationship to God in terms of *sonship*. Indeed, we may say further that his consciousness was of an *intimacy* of sonship which, as embodied in his regular and characteristic address in prayer, 'Abba', still lacks any real parallel among his contemporaries. To that extent Jesus's sense of sonship was something *distinctive*.[12]

All this helps to explain why this short and seemingly ordinary Aramaic word had been preserved amongst Greek-speaking churches. It was remembered as Jesus' strikingly direct way of talking to God and was seen to encapsulate the closeness and confidence of his relationship with God. It is quite likely that '*Abba!* Father!' had already become a familiar feature in the worship of at least some early Christian communities. Certainly it appears to be well known amongst the churches of Galatia as well as in Rome because Paul quotes it in a similar fashion in his letter to them (Gal. 4:6). The way he refers to it on both occasions as a Spirit-inspired cry seems to indicate that it was a common interjection by which people, moved by the Spirit, called out to God in praise and prayer. Paul does not seem to be saying to his readers, that they have been taught to pray according to this liturgical formula in some form of catechetical class. He is probably not even saying that, in learning the Lord's Prayer, they have called God 'Father', even though use of the Lord's Prayer was developing at this time. He seems to be referring to something much more spontaneous and yet, simultaneously, given – the way Christians found themselves praying as the Spirit moved amongst them in gatherings of worship and perhaps also in their personal prayer. To both the Romans and the Galatians Paul uses this liturgical reality as proof of his theological conviction that by faith and baptism Christians have been incorporated into the life of Christ so that, sharing in his righteousness, they participate in his relationship with God as Father, enjoying by adoption the full rights of children of God. With Christ they are 'joint-heirs'. The eschatological promises of God which have been fulfilled in Christ will also be fulfilled in them, on the one condition that they suffer with him, that is that they continue to walk in his way (Rom. 8:17).

Having defined what God has done in the life, death and resurrection of Christ and what God is doing in the lives of believers through their participation in the risen life of Christ, Paul goes on to describe how God will complete his purpose by the work of the Spirit:

> We know that the whole creation has been groaning in labour pains until now; and not only the creation, but we ourselves, who have the first fruits of the Spirit, groan inwardly while

34

we wait for adoption, the redemption of our bodies. For in hope we were saved. Now hope that is seen is not hope. For who hopes for what is seen? But if we hope for what we do not see, we wait for it with patience.

Likewise the Spirit helps us in our weakness; for we do not know how to pray as we ought, but that very Spirit intercedes with sighs too deep for words. And God, who searches the heart, knows what is the mind of the Spirit, because the Spirit intercedes for the saints according to the will of God. (vv. 22–7)

The Spirit who raised Jesus from the dead is the eschatological Spirit, the Spirit of the future which God has prepared for those 'called according to his purpose' (8:28). Paul tells the Christians in Rome that they 'have the first fruits of the Spirit'. Their cry of '*Abba!* Father!' is enough to show that the Spirit of God's new creation in Christ is at work in them, drawing them deeper into the eschatological life of peace with God (5:1) and freedom for life (8:21). But all is not yet complete. Indeed, the work of the Spirit of God's future in them creates a deep longing for the fulfilment of their destiny. As they 'groan inwardly' for the redemption of their bodies, they find themselves caught up with the rest of creation which is also longing, groaning as a woman in labour, for the purposes of God to be fulfilled. Paul sees the human and the non-human creation inextricably bound together – for as the whole of creation has been subjected to the effects of human sin, so humanity cannot enter into its inheritance until the material of creation is made new when the redemption of the body occurs. This time of waiting is not a time for passivity but for prayer. It is the time of intercession in which God's people pray for the coming of God's will. And as they pray they discover that their groaning and the groaning of the rest of creation is none less than the groaning of the eschatological Spirit who yearns for the manifestation of the new creation and so 'intercedes with sighs too deep for words'.

Commentators generally say that Paul is not referring to glossolalia – praying in unknown tongues – at this point.[13] Although they are right in warning against a simple equation of the two, it should be also said that we must avoid missing the experiential and phenomenological step in Paul's argument. Paul's concern is to demonstrate that the Spirit is at work in this time of waiting for the hope to be fulfilled. He wants to show that one way in which the Spirit is at work is in prayer and he does this by referring to the experience of prayer which appears to be common amongst his readers of times in which words fail and, quite literally, deep sighs take over. Paul is saying that this sighing, this welling up within them of such a desire to see the kingdom come that their words cannot contain or express it, is a sign of the Spirit praying within them. Towards the end of the chapter Paul refers also to the intercession of Christ at the right hand of God. Paul's observation and experience is that prayer is not just an activity of the Church as it seeks to relate to God but a dynamic event into which Christians are drawn, as the Spirit moves them, to call out to God as Father in union with the prayer of the ascended Christ. As Robert Jenson puts it:

> the decisive gospel-insight is that if we pray only *to* God, if our relation to God is reducible to the 'to' and is not decisively determined by 'with' and 'in', then it is not the true God whom we identify in our address, but rather some distant and timelessly uninvolved divinity whom we have envisaged. We pray indeed *to* the Father, and so usually address the Father simply as 'God'. But we *address this* Father in that and only in that we pray *with* Jesus *in* their Spirit. The particular God of Scripture does not just stand over against us; he

36

envelops us. And only by the full structure of the envelop-
ment do we have to do with God.[14]

We do not have to claim that Paul had a fully developed
trinitarian theology in which the very being of God is rede-
fined in a threefold way. That would be saying too much.
Some New Testament scholars argue that Paul often used
Christ and the Spirit in interchangeable ways and so had
not developed a full understanding of their ontological
status (their being) and their relationship with each other.
Others maintain that Paul did not even have a concept of
the pre-existence of Christ but saw Jesus as the second Adam
called and sent by God to succeed where the first Adam
failed. We do not have to become embroiled in these
debates because there is no need to establish a formal trinitarian doctrine in Paul's mind. Besides, Paul as a Jewish
Christian theologian was much less interested in questions
of the divine 'being' and much more concerned about
questions of God's action. Indeed, as we said earlier, to
attempt to prove a fully fledged doctrine at this point is
to miss the dynamic of early Christian experience of God.
Romans 8 gives us a significant sight of this dynamic. Most
probably writing sometime between the years 50–3 and
referring to practices which had already become quite established, Paul shows that a trinitarian geography lies at the
heart of the early Christian experience of God's saving
action. God has shown that he is *'for us'* (v. 31) by all that he
has done, is doing and will do in Christ, by the Spirit. This
action of God is *'for us'* even to the extent of being *'in us'*,
enveloping us and including us in a new way of relating to
God. As Gordon Fee says, 'Here is presuppositional Trinitarianism, even if the implications are never addressed by Paul
himself'.[15] One of the collects for Trinity Sunday of the
Church of Rome in our day well expresses the encounter

with God which Paul was trying to explain to the Church of Rome in his day:

> Father, all powerful, Christ the Lord and Saviour,
>   Spirit of love.
> You reveal yourself in the depths of our being,
> drawing us to share in your life and your love.[16]

III THE WORSHIPPING COMMUNITY

The Christian communities depicted in the New Testament were first and foremost *worshipping communities*. Worship was not just an aspect of their corporate lives, it was the essence of their new life in Christ, for their experience of salvation in him was a doxological experience. As we said, doxology means word or speech (*logos*) about glory (*doxa*). It is a category to which we shall be returning in Part Two when we shall be developing its significance for our understanding of trinitarian worship. Suffice it to say at this stage that it refers to the acknowledgement of God's true identity as the one true God, to the experience of the real presence of God and to the transformation which is associated with beholding God's beauty and being in such close proximity to God. We shall look at three descriptions of the Church as a worshipping community in this section.

The first gives us a picture of the Jerusalem Church in its earliest days. Although Luke was writing some years after the events which he describes, there is good reason to think that he reflects the main lines of the earliest community's life:

> They devoted themselves to the apostles' teaching and fellowship, to the breaking of bread and the prayers. Awe came upon everyone, because many wonders and signs were done by the apostles. All who believed were together and had all things in common; they would sell their possessions and

goods and distribute the proceeds to all, as any had need.
Day by day, as they spent much time in the temple, they broke
bread at home and ate their food with glad and generous
hearts, praising God and having the goodwill of all the
people. (Acts 2:42–7)

Although this might sound to us a somewhat idealized
picture, Martin Hengel claims that Luke's account of the
life of the Church in the first chapters of Acts is 'too bland
and too conventional' and goes on to say:

> We know that the first community in Jerusalem was stamped
> in a very elemental way by the primal event, the appearances
> of the risen Christ and the eschatological experience of
> the Spirit. Therefore the worship of the early community
> logically emerged as the work of the Spirit, who inspired the
> Christian prophets to admonitions, 'revelations', visions, but
> also glossolalia. This ecstatic-enthusiastic form of worship
> was not just a new development in the Gentile-Christian
> mission communities, but in my view goes back to the
> beginnings.[17]

Hengel's comment can be best understood when we
appreciate the connection between eschatology and doxology in the biblical framework. Again more attention will
be given to this in Part Two but we need to know at this stage
that the manifestation and accessibility of God's glory was
seen to belong to the *eschaton*, to the end, to the fulfilment
of God's purposes when he would demonstrate finally and
fully that he is the Lord of Lords and King of Kings (e.g. Isa.
2:17, 65:17). We have seen already that the early Christians
believed that this end and fulfilment had happened in the
event of Jesus and that through Christ they had entered into
eschatological salvation, even if only in a provisional and
anticipatory way. Their experience of the glory of God in
worship through the activity of the eschatological Spirit was

proof of the reality of this salvation. Hengel is right when he says that 'This unique eschatological-messianic self-awareness in the first community inevitably burst apart the traditional forms and conventions of worship and created new things'.[18] The direction of the new phenomenon of Christian worship, implicit in the eschatological experience, was trinitarian: the Spirit of the end time had been poured out by God's risen Messiah. As we shall see in the next section, the trinitarian character of the early community's life as reported by Luke in Acts is most clearly seen in its understanding of baptism, but examples of the distinguishable but inseparable experience of Jesus and the Spirit in the life of the early Christian community abound throughout Acts.[19]

The second view of the Christian community comes from the Pauline letters.[20] Here we see the Church in the middle of the first century and now on Gentile soil experiencing a similar form of worship to that of the earliest community in Jerusalem. And we also see them facing some of the problems that this sense of the immediacy of the Spirit and the freedom of their new lives brought to their worship. This is particularly evident at Corinth where the Church was clearly struggling to handle the energy of its worship. Paul helped them to develop ways of understanding themselves as a worshipping community and of ordering their worship. Paul's analysis is intrinsically trinitarian. The criterion for judging whether the spiritual gifts of the community's worship are truly inspired by the Holy Spirit is whether Jesus is being acclaimed as Lord (1 Cor. 12:1–3). The people form the body of Christ and their entry into the body is by the one Spirit (1 Cor. 12:12–13). Within the body of Christ God has appointed each member to play a particular part and equips them by the work of the Spirit:

Now there are varieties of gifts, but the same Spirit;

and there are varieties of services, but the same Lord:
and there are varieties of activities, but it is the same God
who activates all of them in everyone. (1 Cor. 12:4–6)

The third example comes from the letter of Jude. It is often assumed that Jude is of a late composition (the end of the first century or the beginning of the second) and that it represents a time when the charismatic character of the Church's early days was giving way to an emergent catholic order. In fact there are good reasons for saying that although it may well have been written towards the end of the first century, it is addressing a very similar set of problems as those faced by the Pauline communities, except that rather than charismatic excess Jude was clearly confronting charismatic abuse.[21] Itinerant charismatic prophets were disrupting the life of the churches and indulging in unacceptable and immoral behaviour. What is interesting from our point of view is that when Jude exhorts his readers to avoid their contaminating influence, he directs them to the worshipping life of the community (mentioning edification, prayer in the Spirit, love and expectancy for the *parousia*, the coming of Christ) and sets this in a trinitarian framework:

> But you, beloved, build yourselves up on your most holy faith;
> pray in the Holy Spirit; keep yourselves in the love of God;
> look forward to the mercy of our Lord Jesus Christ that leads
> to eternal life. (vv. 20–1)

By remaining firm in the authentic (and apparently trinitarian) pattern of Christian worship, they will be able to withstand the effects of the false teachers.

Dimensions of worship

WORSHIP IN THE SPIRIT

We have already seen how Paul and Jude describe prayer as taking place 'in the Spirit', that is, under the inspiration, guidance and even control of the Spirit of God.[22] In other words prayer is not just a human activity directed towards God, it is directed by God. Geoffrey Wainwright has noted how the Pauline letters describe all the main dimensions of worship as happening 'in the Spirit'.[23] Preaching of the gospel is 'in power and in the Holy Spirit' (1 Thess. 1:5). Baptism is 'in the one Spirit' (1 Cor. 12:13). The confession of Christ as Lord is 'by the Spirit of God' (1 Cor. 12:3). The sealing of Christians for their future redemption is by the 'Holy Spirit' (Eph. 4:30). Paul sees his ministry to the Gentiles as an offering which is 'sanctified by the Holy Spirit' (Rom. 15:16).

The consciousness of worship taking place 'in the Spirit' should be borne in mind when the Spirit is not actually mentioned in other texts which are of a liturgical character, particularly those confessions or credal forms and doxologies which refer only to Christ and God (Rom. 8:34, 1 Cor. 8:5–6, 15:1–7, Rom. 16:25–7, Eph. 3:20–1). Even where there is no explicit reference to the Spirit, it was still understood that the particular ascription of praise or statement of faith could be made only because of the Spirit's presence and work in the worshipping community.

In his massive study on the Spirit in the Pauline letters, Gordon Fee defines the Spirit as 'God's empowering presence'.[24] This is a good paraphrase of what Paul meant by worshipping in the Spirit. Worship can only take place though the enabling and empowering of the Spirit. And the Spirit who enables and empowers is not an impersonal force by which God *acts on* the believers but the eschatological presence of God himself as he *comes to* and *works within* them. Because the Christian community is inhabited by the Spirit, its worship is by definition 'in the Spirit' and yet, because the Christian community is forever dependent upon the Spirit's activity, its worship is marked by a continual openness to the Spirit's inspiration. The relationship between what might be called the *abiding* and the *inspirational* presence of the Spirit will be explored in more detail in Part Two.

SONGS

Songs, often new Christian creations or Christological uses of Jewish psalms, played an important part in the worship of the Christian communities. We find an illuminating description of the role they played in Ephesians 5:18–20:

> Be filled with the Spirit, as you sing psalms and hymns and spiritual songs among yourselves, singing and making melody to the Lord in your hearts, giving thanks to God the Father at all times and for everything in the name of our Lord Jesus Christ.

The overall trinitarian geography of the worship is clear: thanksgiving is made to God the Father in the name of Christ by those who are filled with the Spirit. However, within this pattern some interesting fine details can be observed. The first is that the songs are *spiritual* (*pneumatikos*) – they are inspired by the Spirit. This is probably just as true for psalms and hymns which are more likely to be just different words for liturgical song rather than different categories of song. In a similar passage in the letter to the Colossians it seems that the liturgical song is one way through which the word of Christ becomes present amongst the people.[25] The songs, inspired by the Spirit, are songs about Christ. They give to worship its Christological character. Writing to the Philippians Paul said that Christians are those who 'worship in the Spirit of God and boast of Christ' (Phil. 3:3). The song was one of the ways in which the early Christian communities did so.

Another interesting feature which can be observed from this passage is that if, as seems probable, 'the Lord', to whom melody is made, is Christ, then the songs were not

43

just *about Christ*, they were actually sung *to him*.[26] This raises
the very significant and often neglected issue of the worship
of Christ amongst the first-century communities which we
will be addressing in the next chapter. All we need to note
at this point is that here we can identify a fundamental
difference between the inherited Jewish worship and the
newly developing worship of the Christian community
inspired by the Spirit. Whereas a typical form of Jewish
prayer gave thanks to God for the past event of salvation,
the saving effects of which were being experienced now,
Christian worship gave thanks to God for the past event of
salvation in the consciousness that not only the effects
of salvation in Christ were available to them but that Christ
himself was present to them. In other words, because
Christian salvation was related not just to an *event* through
which God had worked but to a *person* through whom God
was still working, Christian worship could not be expressed
simply by reference to him but had to include a relationship
with him. Nevertheless, the relationship with Christ was
such that it did not direct people away from God but rather
drew them into the closest possible contact with him. The
melody which was made to Christ did not end with Christ,
it was always moving beyond him towards the Father in
thanksgiving. Similarly the purpose of the confession of
Christ as Lord at the end of the hymn in Philippians 2 was
for the glory of God the Father.

THANKSGIVING

Essentially the song was a eucharistic song, a song of thanksgiving, the groundswell of the joy of the Christian
community as it celebrated the eschatological salvation to
be found in Christ. Indeed, Christians are essentially
eucharistic people, people of thanksgiving whose lives are
marked by a deep sense of gratitude for their salvation
in Christ (Col. 2:7). Also the worshipping community is

essentially a eucharistic community, a community of thanks-giving in which its whole life, even its prayers of supplication, is marked by grateful praise (Col. 3:15; 1 Thess. 5:18). The second letter to the Thessalonians provides us with an example of how the prayer of thanksgiving naturally took on a threefold form: thanks are given to God for saving the Thessalonian Christians by the sanctifying work of the Spirit and by their belief in the truth of Christ (2 Thess. 2:13).

The eucharistic character of the early Christian community came to its clearest expression as it celebrated the Lord's Supper:

> The cup of blessing which we bless, is it not a sharing in the blood of Christ? The bread that we break, is it not a sharing in the body of Christ? Because there is one bread, we who are many are one body. (1 Cor. 10:16–17)

The cup of blessing in any Jewish meal, and particularly in the Passover, was the cup over which thanksgiving for the wine was given. It was a symbol of the blessings God had poured out upon his covenant people Israel and a way of sharing in them. Now, in the Christian meal, the cup of blessing is the cup over which thanksgiving is given for the new covenant available to all people (11:25). As the cup is passed around the new community, so its members share in the blessings of Christ's saving death. The bread which was broken and shared in any Jewish meal, and particularly in the Passover, was an affirmation of the people's member-ship of the covenant community. The bread which Christians break together and share with each other is the affirmation and confirmation of their place in the new community of the body of Christ.

Although the Spirit is not explicitly related to the Lord's Supper by Paul, it is not difficult to see the implicit connec-tions between the Spirit and the Supper in the early Christian experience, especially when we remember that all worship was seen as taking place 'in the Spirit'. Luke tells us how the earliest Christian community broke bread 'with jubilation' (*en agalliasei*) (Acts 2:46). Jubilation was an eschatological characteristic. In the Septuagint, the Greek translation of the Old Testament, the same word was used frequently in the Psalms to describe deep rejoicing in God's saving action. Elsewhere in the New Testament it is used to express the exaltation of the Christian people as they await the coming of Christ (1 Pet. 1:8) and as they anticipate the marriage feast of the Lamb (Rev. 19:7). We have seen how the earliest Christian community viewed its experience of the Spirit as proof that eschatological salvation had come. Putting all this together we can say that a profound sense of joy was felt as the community gathered to break bread in the name of Christ. Here the salvation brought by the Spirit was experienced both in the new depth of fellowship which believers shared with each other and in the new form of fellowship with God which, until then, had been part of the prophetic promise but had now become part of the Church's practice.

If Acts gives us an example of the Spirit confirming the community in the reality of eschatological salvation through the bread it shared together, Paul gives us evidence of the Spirit calling the community to long for its fulfilment as it celebrated the Lord's Supper. He tells the Corinthians that by eating the bread and drinking the cup they 'proclaim the Lord's death until he comes' (1 Cor. 11:26). According to Jeremias, the phrase 'until he comes' plays on the cry of *maranatha* which, as Paul shows at the end of the letter, had become a familiar invocation in early Christian worship (1 Cor. 16:22). *Maranatha* is an aramaic expression meaning 'O Lord, come'. Like *Abba* it had been preserved amongst Greek-speaking congregations because it was seen to express something of the essence of Christian existence – in this case the yearning of the Spirit within the community for the fullness of Christ's kingdom. Jeremias says that 'this proclamation expressed the vicarious death of Jesus as the beginning of the salvation time and prays for the coming of the consummation'.[27]

So we can see that the Lord's Supper was celebrated with a trinitarian perspective. The people gave thanks to God, they participated in the body of Christ and the Spirit filled them with both the joy of tasting God's kingdom and the longing for its coming on earth as in heaven.

PRAYER FOR THE BELIEVERS, CONFESSION OF CHRIST AND
DOXOLOGIES

Just as the prayer of thanks for the faith of believers took on a trinitarian shape, so the prayers for their continual growth in faith were expressed in a trinitarian form. When praying for the Ephesian Christians Paul asks the Father that they may be strengthened through the Spirit and that Christ may dwell in their hearts by faith (Eph. 3:14–16; see also Eph. 1:17–22, Col. 1:9–13).

In the Pauline letters, and elsewhere in the New Testament, material of an expressly confessional kind can be found. Here Paul is either articulating Christian faith in a summary form or quoting an existing credal formula which would have been familiar in the worship of the communities to whom he was writing. We have already indicated that most of these refer to Christ and God and do not explicitly mention the Spirit. In many ways that is just what we would expect. The early Christians believed that they had been redeemed by God's decisive action in Christ. The task of the embryonic Christian theology was to make sense of the significance of Christ in the purposes of God. The role of credal formulae was to confess this significance before God. But the early Christian communities knew that their life and faith were lived in the power of the Spirit and that the Spirit was enabling their confession of Christ to be made with

47

deeper conviction and increasing clarity. We shall discover as we journey beyond the New Testament that although *trinitarian* rather than *binitarian* theology is made necessary by the distinct and particular activity of the Spirit, it is made difficult by the nature of the Spirit's work which is always to focus on the Son and on the Father rather than to remain in the spotlight of attention.

Nevertheless, Paul does provide us with a very interesting example of a credal formula which mentions the Spirit as well as God and Christ:

> the gospel concerning his Son, who was descended from David according to the flesh and was declared to be Son of God with power according to the spirit of holiness by resurrection from the dead, Jesus Christ our Lord. (Rom. 1:3–4)

It is likely that the central section of these words formed an early, pre-Pauline credal statement which, if we follow C.K. Barrett, is better translated:

> in the sphere of the flesh, born of the family David;
> in the sphere of the Holy Spirit, appointed Son of God.[28]

This expresses the basic Christian conviction that although Jesus was fully rooted in human life and Jewish ancestry, he was equally related to the divine life (see also 1 Tim. 3:16). Although a Son of David he was also, because of the Spirit's action upon and through him, Son of God.

The poetic structure of the creed suggests that its original setting was in song. In the light of what was said about the use of songs in early Christian worship, it is quite possible that here we can see an example of how Christian liturgical formulae evolved. An utterance of a Spirit-inspired worshipper was remembered, repeated and circulated amongst a number of communities and so became a fixed liturgical form which could be used in both worship and catechism.

Like most of the confessional or credal material, the doxologies – bursts of praise to God – which can be found in the New Testament, do not explicitly refer to the Spirit. However, they are interesting from our point of view because, given that Christian worship by definition took place 'in the Spirit', the doxologies reveal the trinitarian movement which we observed when discussing the use of songs in Christian worship. The basic thrust is towards God the Father but the praise is given because of the work of Christ. Hence, it was offered *through* Christ, and in some cases Christ is associated in the closest possible way with the glory given to God (Rom. 11:33–6, Eph. 3:20–1, Rom. 16:25–7). There are three examples of doxologies addressed directly to Christ (2 Tim. 4:18; 2 Pet. 3:18; Rev. 1:5–6) but as they appear in books which are generally felt to be later than the material we have been considering in this chapter, we will hold them over until the next chapter.

BAPTISM

Peter's answer to the crowd who were calling out to know what they must do to be saved gives us the main ingredients of the early Christian understanding of baptism:

> Repent and be baptized every one of you in the name of Jesus Christ so that your sins may be forgiven; and you will receive the gift of the Holy Spirit. For the promise is for you, for your children, and for all who are far away, everyone whom the Lord our God calls to him. (Acts 2:38–9)

First baptism involves repentance, a complete reorientation towards Christ and an acceptance of him as God's Messiah through whom the Spirit has now been sent. Second, baptism is in the 'name of Christ'. In practice this probably meant that as people were baptized they would call out the name of Christ (Acts 22:16). It may have also involved the congregation invoking Christ's name as the baptism took place (Acts 15:17; Jas. 2:7). In baptism people identified Christ as their Saviour and themselves as his followers. They were being baptized *into* the name Christ – into the way of Christ, the community of Christ, into the life lived in, with and through Christ. Third, the baptism brought with it the forgiveness of sins – God's eschatological gift of the New Covenant. Fourth, because baptism was an initiation into the eschatological life it had to involve the coming of the Spirit. The trinitarian pattern is again clear. Baptism is a dynamic event in which through the past work and continuing presence of Christ and by the activity of the Spirit believers are established in a new fellowship with God – a fellowship once promised but now present.[29]

Further evidence of the Church's trinitarian experience of baptism can be found in the narratives of Jesus' baptism in the Gospels. There was a reciprocal relationship of influence between the baptism narratives and the practice of the early Christian communities. The memory of Jesus' baptism in the tradition of the Church would have clearly affected the way baptism was practised. On the other hand, the Church's practice of baptism inevitably helped to shape the narratives and to provide their theological perspective. As Jesus is baptized, the Father speaks his word claiming Jesus as his Son and the Spirit descends on him. Just as Jesus' prayer to God as *Abba* was the source and model of Christian prayer in the Spirit to God, so his baptism was the source and model of Christian baptism in the Spirit. As in their prayer they shared in his prayer, so in their baptism they shared in his baptism. By the work of the Spirit they became children of the Father. Matthew shows us that by the time he wrote his Gospel the trinitarian character of Christian identity was made explicit in Christian initiation through the use of the trinitarian formula:

'Go therefore and make disciples of all nations, baptizing

them in the name of the Father and of the Son and of the Holy Spirit, and teaching them to obey everything that I have commanded you. And remember, I am with you always, to the end of the age.' (Matt. 28:19–20)

IV SOME CONCLUDING REFLECTIONS

The triadic pattern of early Christian worship is given classic expression in the letter to the Ephesians:

> So he [Christ] came and proclaimed peace to you who were far off and peace to those who were near, for through him both of us have access in one Spirit to the Father. (2:17–18)
>
> In him the whole structure is joined together and grows into a holy temple in the Lord; in whom you also are built together spiritually [*en pneumati*] into a dwelling place for God. (2:21–2)

Combining the imagery of the temple and the body Paul defines Christian salvation in terms of doxological privilege. The temple in Jerusalem was divided into various courts in which Gentiles and Jews, Jewish men and women, Jewish laymen and priests had their respective places in graded degrees of relation to the presence of God. Only the high priest was admitted into the holy of holies and then only once a year – on the day of Atonement when he came bearing the blood of the sacrifice for sin. Now, says Paul, the way into this holiest place of God's dwelling has been opened for all through the sacrifice of Christ. But it is not just a case of one more effective sacrifice replacing another less effective one. It is that the temple itself has been relocated and, in one sense, is still being erected. It is now to be found in the new humanity of Christ into which both Gentiles and Jews are being built by the Spirit. The God who is encountered in this holy place is the God of Jesus, the one Jesus called with tender love, *Abba*. This is the one they have to do with when, by the work of the Spirit, they come to Christ. And the Spirit who gathers them into Christ not only carries them into the real presence of God but also brings the real presence of God to them (see also 1 Cor. 3:16–17, 2 Cor. 6:16). Even now, by his Spirit, God is dwelling with his people. The long-awaited hope that God would be present in the midst of his people has happened (Ezek. 37:27). The experience of the eschatological presence of God in the worship of the early Christian communities, could not be separated from the experience of Christ and the Spirit, because it was only in, by and through their present activity that God was known, loved and, in the deepest sense, enjoyed.

3

The Pattern, Precedents and Perspectives of
Worship in the New Testament

> *They are before the throne of God*
> *and worship him day and night*
> *within his temple.*
>> *(Revelation 7:15)*

I INTRODUCTION

In the last chapter we saw that as the early Christian communities gathered to worship in Jerusalem, Ephesus, Rome
and elsewhere – meeting of course in people's homes, often
under fear of persecution – they sang hymns in honour of
Christ, baptized new believers and shared meals in his name,
gave thanks to God because of Christ and confessed him as
Lord. Their experience of salvation, made tangible by the
presence and power of the Spirit amongst them, was centred
on the person of Jesus, born of Mary, crucified by Pilate and
raised to new life by God. In this chapter we shall look more
closely at the part played by Jesus in the worship of the early
Christians. This will help us to see the shape and colour of
Christian worship more clearly because it is this which gave
Christian worship its distinctive pattern. We shall then look
beyond the pattern to see if we can discern something of
the background onto which it was woven. Were there any
structures and assumptions, conventions and expectations

in the contemporary Jewish spirituality which formed some sort of sympathetic environment for the development of the role of Jesus in early Christian worship? Finally we shall move on to look at three quite sophisticated theologies within the New Testament which reveal the fabric of Christian worship in various perspectives and with different shades of subtlety.

II PATTERN: WORSHIP OF JESUS[1]

Prayer to Jesus

Prayer to Christ is assumed to be normal Christian practice in both Acts and in Paul's letters. At the beginning of Acts Luke shows the relationship which the disciples enjoyed with the risen Christ who came amongst them as they met together (1:6–8), continues in their gatherings after his ascension. Before the ascension they ask him a straight question, 'Lord, is this the time when you will restore the kingdom to Israel?' After the ascension, when they are trying to choose a successor to Judas, they ask Jesus another direct question, though this time in prayer: 'Lord, you know everyone's heart. Show us . . .' (1:24). Luke indicates that visionary experiences of Christ may have played a formative part in the development of prayer to Christ. Stephen at his death, Paul in his conversion, Ananias in Damascus all speak directly to the Lord whom they see in their visions (7:59–60; 9:3–6; 9:10–17). Paul's own writings reinforce this impression. In 2 Corinthians 12:1–10 Paul recounts a particularly intense religious experience in which he received 'visions and revelations from the Lord' (v. 1) and conversed with Christ (vv. 8–9).

Another example of Paul's attitude about prayer to Christ can be seen in the greetings which begin and the benedictions ending his letters. Invariably they invoke the grace of

Christ upon his hearers. Often the greeting is from 'God the Father and our Lord Jesus Christ' and sometimes the benediction simply commends the grace of Christ to the churches. It is quite likely that these were commonplace expressions in the worship of the communities to which Paul was writing. And it seems probable that Paul understood them to be a précis of the sort of prayer he prays in 1 Thessalonians 3:11–13:

> Now may our God and Father himself and our Lord Jesus direct our way to you. And may the Lord make you increase and abound in love for one another and for all, just as we abound in love for you. And may he also strengthen your hearts in holiness that you may be blameless before our God and Father at the coming of our Lord Jesus with all the saints.

As Paul envisaged that his prayer would be answered by God (the Father) and Christ (the Lord) we can assume that his prayer was addressed as much to one as to the other.

A further example of direct prayer to Christ in the worship of the first Christian communities is the *maranatha* invocation. This widely-known Aramaic term originated amongst the earliest Palestinian Jewish Christians and remained untranslated amongst later Greek-speaking churches. As we saw in the last chapter it was a direct petition to Christ, naming him as Lord and calling on him to come with the fullness of eschatological salvation (literally 'our Lord, come'). As with the Greek *kyrios,* the ascription of the Aramaic *marêh* did not in itself ascribe divine lordship to Christ. Both could be used as respectful addresses without any implication of divinity. But we must remember the contexts in which Jesus was called Lord. They were the settings of worship. In Jewish thought and life the practice of worship was the examination room for monotheism. If Jesus was being called Lord in the context of worship and prayed to as a source of divine help from the earliest days of the Church, then the definition of the one God had already taken on a distinctively Christian form.

Calling on the name of Jesus

In the last chapter we saw that Jesus' name was called upon during baptisms and that he was confessed as Lord in worship. We now need to explore the theological significance of these liturgical practices a little more closely. We can do so by looking at Paul's Damascus Road experience, first as told by Luke in Acts and then as alluded to by Paul in his letters.

In Acts 9 we hear that Saul of Tarsus, the devout Jew, was on his way to Damascus to arrest those who called upon the name of Jesus, Ananias amongst them. The issue for Paul was not that Ananias and his friends were claiming allegiance to the figure and teaching of Jesus as, for example, a Marxist might call on the name of Marx, but that they were calling on the name of Jesus *as if they were calling on the name of YHWH, Israel's God.* To set the context we need to go back to Peter's speech on the Day of Pentecost in Acts 2. Here he claimed that the disciples' overwhelming experience of the Spirit earlier on that morning was the fulfilment of Joel's prophecy that, 'in the last days', God would pour out his Spirit on all flesh. The day of eschatological salvation had now come in which 'all who call upon the name of the Lord will be saved' (2:17–21). Peter went on to speak of the life, death, resurrection and ascension of Jesus and then ended with the proclamation that God has made this Jesus 'Lord and Christ' (2:36). Luke tells us that the listeners were deeply moved and called out, 'what must we do to be saved?' Peter responded by giving them the old answer ('you must call upon the name of the Lord') in a new form – 'You must repent and every one of you must be baptized *in the name of the Lord Jesus* for the forgiveness of sins' (2:38).

The logic was clear. YHWH's name is YHWH's presence and power. The promise is that on the day of salvation YHWH will save those who call upon him. The day of promise will be the day of the pouring out of the Spirit. This was the Jewish world view. But Peter presented the new world view of the fledgling Christian community. The time had come. The Spirit was being poured out. The day of salvation, the day of the forgiveness of sins, had arrived for those who would call upon the one in whom the Lordship of YHWH was being manifested. In other words, because of God's eschatological action in Christ, the way to call upon the name of YHWH was by calling on the name of Christ. In fact, in the purposes of God, Christ is the Lord.

Luke shows us that this is what Paul discovered on the way to Damascus. He is at pains to show that rather than betraying Israel's God, as Paul had thought, the people who call upon the name of Jesus are those who have experienced the fulfilment of God's covenant promises. Paul's vision comes from God. It is as much from God as Ezekiel's vision of the dazzling brightness of God's glory in the temple, for like the prophet Paul falls to the ground and hears a voice (Ezek. 1:28). Paul's vision is not opposed to the purposes of God, it simply explains how God is working out his purposes. It shows that God has made Jesus the Lord through whom salvation is to be found. Luke spells this out more clearly in the third account of Paul's testimony in which we hear the risen Christ applying one of Isaiah's Servant Songs telling of the coming salvation to himself (26:9–18 and Isa. 42).

When we turn to the allusions to Paul's conversion in his letters we can see that Luke has accurately presented the main lines of Paul's experience and that they share a similar understanding of the event. In 2 Corinthians 3:4–4:6, where

Paul compares the giving of the Law through Moses and the coming of the gospel in Christ, he seems to be drawing on his Damascus experience. He refers to the *light* of the glory of Christ, 'the image of God', and to the glory of God *shining* in the face of Christ. In a biographical section of Galatians Paul describes how the gospel came to him through a 'revelation of Jesus Christ' in which God 'chose to reveal his Son' to him and commissioned him to preach to the Gentiles. Of course we do not know what theological connections Paul actually made at the time of the vision but we do know that his sight of the risen and exalted Christ (1 Cor. 9:1) shattered his existing world view and initiated him into the Christian conviction that in Christ we are confronted with the presence and power of God.

In Romans 10:5–13 we see him working this through systematically and arriving at the same conclusions as Luke weaved into his narrative. Paul shows that we are saved by declaring, on the basis of our belief in the resurrection, that Jesus is Lord. In support he quotes Joel's prophecy that all those who call upon the name of the Lord will be saved. Again the logic is clear. The promise is fulfilled. Salvation from God is here. It is here in Christ. And Christ is not only the bringer of salvation but also in some sense the giver of salvation, for God has chosen Christ's name to be counted as his name: YHWH's sacred name is shared with Christ.

Hymns[2]

Christians sang of their salvation from the earliest days. In a similar pattern to the narrative psalms of their Jewish worship they told the story of their salvation in praise of God. The central theme of their story was of course Jesus Christ and, in particular, his saving death and his heavenly exaltation:

> Christ, though he was in the form of God,

58

did not count equality with God
as something to be exploited,
but emptied himself,
taking the form of a slave,
being born in human likeness.
And being found in human form,
he humbled himself and became obedient to the point
of death –
even death on a cross.
Therefore God also highly exalted him
and gave him the name that is above every name,
so that at the name of Jesus every knee should bend,
in heaven and earth and under the earth,
and every tongue confess that Jesus Christ is Lord
to the glory of God the Father. (Phil. 2:6–11)

This pre-Pauline hymn which Paul quotes as part of his wider argument is one of the best examples of an early Christian hymn to be found in the New Testament. But it is quite probable that we have up to sixty other fragments quoted in different parts of the New Testament writings.[3] Philippians 2:6–11 helps us to see that Christian hymns about Christ functioned in a different way from Jewish psalms about, for example, the Exodus. The nature of God's saving work in Christ is that the person of Christ is included within the orbit of praise which is given to God. God raises Jesus on high and gives him the name above all names so that all creation will bow the knee to Christ in homage and confess him as Lord. Yes the hymn looks forward to the final consummation of all things but given all that we have said about the significance of the name of Christ and the Lordship of Christ in the present experience of the early Christians, it would seem that the hymn implies worship of Jesus as much now as then.

Further support can be found in Ephesians 5:19 which, as

we saw in the last chapter, tells the believers to sing to Christ and in Hebrews 1 where the writer provides a series of quotations from the Psalms which are likely to have been familiar elements in the worship of at least some Christian communities. The writer assumes that two of the psalms (45:6–7 and 102:25–7) are addressed to Christ himself, indicating that singing songs to Christ in praise of him was seen as a normal and acceptable liturgical practice. Finally, the visions described in the book of Revelation picture the worship of heaven in which Christ is included in the praise which is given to God:

'Worthy is the Lamb that was slaughtered
to receive power and wealth and wisdom and might
and honour and glory and blessing!' (5:12)

'To the one seated on the throne and to the Lamb
be blessing and honour and glory and might
for ever and ever!' (5:13)

We shall focus more fully on Revelation at the end of the chapter and so at this point we need simply to note that John regards the worship of Jesus in song as a proper part of the worship of God and as an intrinsic element in the experience of eschatological salvation which lay at the root of the 'new song' (Rev. 5:9) of the early Christian communities as they gathered 'in the Spirit' to give thanks and praise.

Doxologies

Doxologies were a common feature of Jewish worship. They ascribed glory to the one God, the God of Israel, and were often included in letters as well as prayers and sermons. As we saw in the last chapter, they took on a Christian form by being offered *through Christ*. However, 2 Timothy 4:18, 2 Peter 3:18, and Revelation 1:5–6 provide three unambiguous examples from different geographical areas and theological traditions of doxologies directed just to Christ. For example:

> The Lord will rescue me from every attack and save me for his heavenly kingdom. To him be the glory for ever and ever. Amen. (2 Tim. 4:18)

The letter begins with a greeting of 'grace, mercy and peace from our Father and from Christ Jesus our Lord' (1:2), repeatedly refers to salvation in and through Christ (2:10, 3:15) and includes a solemn charge 'in the presence of God and of Christ Jesus, who is to judge the living and the dead' (4:1). It is not then surprising that it ends with an ascription of the praise which belongs to God, for Christ was seen to belong to God and to be the one through whom God acted and in whom God could be found.

Direct references to the worship of Jesus

In Acts 13:2 Luke describes the prophets and teachers at Antioch 'worshipping [*leitourgountôn*] the Lord and fasting'. The verb *leitourgein* was part of the vocabulary of Jewish worship and referred to various religious practices in the service of God. The indication here is that Christ had become the focus of the liturgy – the service – of the Christians at Antioch.

Luke uses *proskynein*, a stronger verb, at the end of his Gospel when he tells us that immediately after Christ ascended to heaven the disciples: 'worshipped [*proskynēsantes*] him, and returned to Jerusalem with great joy, and they were continually in the temple blessing God' (24:52–3). *Proskynein* meant to prostrate oneself out of homage or reverence. It could be used to signify the respect given to another person of a higher social standing (e.g. Matt. 18:26) but in the Greek version of the Jewish Scriptures (the Septuagint) it was used in relation to divine worship and in

61

the book of Hebrews it clearly referred to divine adoration (e.g. 1:6, 11:21). Luke's usage is deliberate and calculated. In the temptation narratives he had made it clear that such homage could be made only to God (4:5–8). Now, he says, it can be offered to the one whom God has raised from the grave and exalted to his right hand (see Acts 2:34–6). Luke began his Gospel with the scene of Zechariah serving God in the temple awaiting the deliverance of Israel (1:5–20, 67–79). He ended it with the scene of the disciples worshipping the one in whom the deliverance had come and then returning to the temple.

Whereas Luke referred only to the risen and ascended Christ being worshipped, Matthew gives several examples of people bowing down in worship before him: the Magi (2:2,8,11), those seeking his healing powers (8:2, 9:18, 15:25) and the women at the empty tomb (28:9). Matthew obviously wanted to make clear that this is the proper attitude which people should have towards Jesus. In so doing he was reflecting the practice of the early Christian communities who knew that Christ was present amongst them as they gathered together and welcomed him with wonder and worship (18:20, 28:20).

Just as Luke and Matthew allowed Christ to be worshipped *and* affirmed that worship belongs only to God, the book of Revelation also restricted worship only to God (19:10b, 22:8–9) *and* extended the worship of the one God to include the worship of Jesus (4:9–5:14). The critical point to bear in mind about Matthew and Revelation in particular is that they are both thoroughly Jewish-Christian documents and are therefore noticeably sensitive to basic Jewish religious assumptions and principles. Indeed, Revelation was written as a protest against the idolatry of the beast demanded by Roman imperialism and as a call to be faithful to the one true God.

In the scholarly study of the New Testament and the

development of Christian doctrine it was fashionable for many years to argue that the worship of Jesus was imported into Christianity by pagan converts. It was claimed that the converts brought with them not only much more blurred understandings of divinity than were found in Hebrew religion, but also versions of what has been dubbed 'the divine-redeemer myth' – a collection of beliefs about a semi-divine figure who came out of heaven, redeemed the people, returned to heaven and was worshipped as a result.[4] Studies over recent years, however, have seriously undermined such views. It has become increasingly accepted that the risen and exalted Christ assumed a place of divine significance in the religious experience of Christians from the earliest days of the movement, and that the worship of Christ was defended and commended in Jewish Christian communities by those who retained and maintained the proper Hebrew concern for the worship of God alone.[5] In fact, it has been suggested that Christian beliefs about Jesus acted as a catalyst for speculation about the dealings of the divine with the world and may have been a cause, rather than a consequence, of stories and theories about a redeemer figure in the contemporary religion of the time.[6]

Hence in conclusion we should underline that the early Christians did not worship Jesus as a competing divine figure alongside their worship of the God of their Jewish faith. To do so would have been to attempt to share YHWH's glory with another (Isa. 42:8) and so deny their monotheistic inheritance. Rather the pattern of their experience of salvation became the pattern of their worship of God. In the new world of eschatological salvation the worship of God took place in the Spirit through the presence, power, mediation and mercy of Christ to the glory of God the Father (Phil. 2:11). God could no longer be worshipped without reference to the person of Jesus. Christ had become a co-ordinate in the divine worship of the one God.

III PRECEDENTS: JEWISH BACKGROUND

In the last section we established that Jesus very soon assumed a place of divine significance in the religious experience of the early Christian communities. Relating to God in prayer and praise, love and worship, involved relating to Jesus. Receiving from God in word and sign, healing and forgiveness, involved receiving from Jesus. Jesus was there in the holy place – the God place – not in isolation from or in competition with the God of their history, but *as the appointed place* in which the God of Israel could be found. The question we must now face is whether this belief that Christ had been exalted into the holy place, the place of the lordship of YHWH, represented a denial of the basic conviction upon which the people of YHWH based their lives:

> Hear, O Israel: The Lord [YHWH] our God,
> the Lord [YHWH] is one. (Deut. 6:4)

These are the words of the *Shema* which were etched into the corporate memory and identity of the Jewish people. We can be fairly sure that Jesus and his early followers brought up in Jewish homes of the first century would have recited the *Shema* at a number of points in the day as part of their family prayers. But as Rabbi Isidore Epstein insists, we do not have an 'assertion here of the unity of God in the metaphysical sense'.[7] Rather we have in the *Shema*, as the New Testament scholar Tom Wright puts it, 'the battle cry of the nation', a 'fighting doctrine'[8] of a people who believed that their God was the only God and that his lordship over all would one day become manifestly clear – the day when he established justice, mercy, healing and forgiveness. On that day, the day of YHWH, the eschatological day, all nations would acknowledge YHWH as Lord and worship him alone. Tom Wright concludes his detailed survey of the nature of Jewish monotheism in the first century by saying: 'Within the most fiercely monotheistic circles throughout our period . . . there is no suggestion that "monotheism" or praying the *Shema*, had anything to do with the numerical analysis of the inner being of Israel's god himself. It had everything to do with the two-pronged fight against paganism and dualism.'[9] Paganism, with its belief in several gods, and dualism, with its belief in two ultimate sources, good and evil, both denied Israel's conviction that her God was the only Lord of heaven and earth and that his purposes would triumph.

By stressing that monotheism in the first century was a statement about the *supremacy* rather than the *simplicity* of God, I am not trying to soften the apparent scandal of the place of Jesus in early Christian devotion. Indeed, as I suggested earlier, the practice of worship was the examination room in the school of monotheism. The basis of Jewish religion – as the Ten Commandments made clear – was that worship was to be offered to YHWH alone because YHWH alone is the creator and ruler of all things. I am simply trying to focus on the right question. The central issue is what constitutes the lordship of the one God – or, to put it another way, how the Lord, the one God, is constituted as God. The worship of Jesus indicates that for the early Jewish Christians the constitution of God – the way God shows himself to be in his revelation and redemption – includes, in some sense, the person of Jesus.

We move on to look briefly at some of the images and categories circulating in the culture of Jewish religion at this time which were trying to make sense of God's revelation and redemption. These will help us to see that although there was a radical newness about the Christian experience of salvation which led to a genuinely new turning in the worship of God, all sorts of other roads were being travelled in contemporary Jewish spirituality which helped pave the way.

The Hebrew understanding of the lordship of God involved believing that God is both *beyond the world* and present *within the world.* As the creator, God cannot be confined within all that he has brought into being. God transcends the world. However, God's transcendence over the world is not expressed in *absence* from the world but in *activity* within the world. God has loved the creation into being and committed himself to fashion it according to his purposes. Jewish religion therefore claimed that while God was not *of the world,* he was most certainly *in the world.* Finding a theologically proper and spiritually satisfying way of describing both convictions had always been the particular challenge of Jewish theology and spirituality. It became a more prominent concern in the period after the return from exile in Babylon. By the first century it had become a major preoccupation. We shall touch upon a number of attempts to express God's relation to the world. They can be clustered around three headings: attributes, figures and temple.

Attributes[10]

By the first century a number of God's attributes had become personified. Wisdom and Word are two of the most important. In the book of Proverbs Wisdom is pictured as a personal being created by God at 'the beginning of his work' (8:22) who calls the people to find and follow her ways (1:20–33; 8:32–6). As the post-exilic moves on into the intertestamental period, Wisdom becomes 'the breath of the power of God' (7:26). She is both the 'designer of all things' (7:21) and the one who 'renews the world' (7:27). Knowing the will of God (9:9–11), she delivered the people from slavery in Egypt (10:15–11:2). Similarly, the Word of

God became increasingly personalized as Jewish thought developed. The Word which YHWH spoke to the prophets began to be described in more independent terms. In Isaiah 55 God sends his word from heaven and says that it will not 'return to him empty' – it will effect his purposes. In the Wisdom of Solomon, written in the first century BCE, the Word leaps from heaven and stands in Egypt as a 'stern warrior' wielding the judgement of God (18:14–16). By about the time of Christ, the Jewish philosopher Philo was describing the Word as a 'mediator', as God's firstborn and even as 'a second God'.

In the light of such language about the Wisdom and the Word it is hardly surprising that many scholars have concluded that by the first century another divine entity was believed to exist alongside God and therefore that Jewish monotheism had been already seriously compromised. This is an unnecessary conclusion. In one way the giving of a personal character to the attributes of God was simply a way of envisaging the action of God more easily. By personalizing the presence and activity of God, Jewish tradition was able to picture it more fully and more accurately. Jewish faith believed that God was personal. Therefore his way of relating to his people had to be expressed in personal terms. Beyond this, language about God's Wisdom and Word was an attempt to express the belief that God was active in the world but was not contained within the confines of the world. By talking in terms of God's Wisdom and Word, Jewish tradition was able to say that God was immanent in the world while at the same time maintain that God was transcendent to the world – for although the Word and Wisdom were the presence of God in action, they were not the totality of his presence. The Wisdom and Word belonged to God and yet God was beyond them, just as our wisdom and words are intrinsic to us but not identical with us. We are more than our wisdom and our words.

Jewish faith remained thoroughly monotheistic. Neither the Wisdom nor the Word were seen as separate deities but as the personal presence and action of God in relation to his creation. Nevertheless, the use made of them by the time of the first century indicates that the one God was conceived of in ways which allowed for some form of plurality or distinction within God.

Figures[11]

In an important study Larry Hurtado argues that as well as being an example of the personalization of the attributes of God, the later Jewish use of Wisdom and Word was part of an increasing tendency to see God acting through an agent or servant who represents God and acts on his behalf, as a vice-regent does for a monarch or an ambassador for a nation. He then goes on to show how Jewish thought projected a number of different patriarchal and angelic figures into the role of the chief agent of God. Enoch was believed to have been exalted to heaven where he acted as God's judge and stood as the vizier or head of the royal court. Traditions about Moses also saw him enthroned in heaven and described him as the mediator of the covenant. He was seen as God's representative and as God's instrument. Philo even described him as God's 'partner' in the sense of sharing certain divine qualities. Other patriarchal figures such as Abraham and Jacob were also given an exalted and representative status and Adam was the subject of a developing mythology.

A similarly mediatorial role was given to Gabriel, Michael, Raphael and other angelic beings. Different traditions identified a particular angel as the recipient of God's authority and as a sharer, in some sense, in God's glory. The angel could manifest the presence of God, communicate a message from God and battle for God's purposes. Most striking is the figure of Yahoel. It seems that he was seen as the embodiment of God's name. In the Apocalypse of Abraham he was described in language which formerly had been used only of God.

A critical difference, however, between the human and angelic figures on the one hand and the Wisdom and Word on the other is that the former were appointments of God whereas the latter were expressions of God.[12] The attributes belonged to God. The figures were delegated by God to fulfil particular functions or roles. One proof of their creaturely status was that the figures were never regarded as worthy of worship. The worship of Jesus amongst Christians still on the soil of Palestinian Judaism shows that the early Christians instinctively believed that Christ was in a different order to any human or angelic mediator of Jewish tradition. He belonged, as Paul said, to God (1 Cor. 3:23). Nevertheless, although the agents of God's purposes in Jewish tradition did not anticipate the full role Jesus played in Christian theology and spirituality, the expectation that God would act through a mediating human figure was a suggestive and sympathetic element in the early Christian inherited world view which helped the first Christians to make sense of Jesus.

Temple[13]

In Jewish theology and practice the temple functioned as a point at which the transcendent God of all creation made himself available and even visible to his covenant people. Temple theology had its origins in the Tent of Meeting in which YHWH dwelt with his people and travelled with them as they journeyed to the promised land. It was the place of encounter with God, of blessing from and for God and of the manifestation of God (Lev. 9:23–4). The Tent housed the ark of the covenant and so embodied the covenant relationship between YHWH and his people. YHWH had committed himself to Israel and demanded loyalty from his people in return.

These themes were taken over into the actual temple of Jerusalem built during the reign of Solomon in the tenth century BCE. The temple was a place of worship. YHWH was available to his people through prayer and sacrifice. Here the Lord could be blessed by his people and the people blessed by him (Ps. 143). It was a place of presence. God filled the temple with his glory (Ps. 26:8, 1 Kings 8:10–13) and made himself accessible to those who would seek his face (Ps. 27). The temple was a place of salvation. People fled to the temple for refuge and the temple assured them that God would overthrow their enemies (Ps. 48). In the words of the Jewish theologian Jon Levenson the temple was 'the visible form, the "incarnation", so to speak, of the sacred story of YHWH's commitment to rescue those loyal to him'.[14] Accordingly, the temple was the place of the covenant. As the home of the ark of the covenant it was the sign both of God's covenant faithfulness and of Israel's obligation to maintain her obedience to the demands of the covenant.

The tendency amongst many to treat the temple as an unconditional guarantee of God's favour regardless of their ethical and religious life added fuel to the fires of the prophetic protest against any form of covenant disobedience. Jeremiah spoke vehemently against those who smoothly assured the people that the mere presence of the temple falsified his prophecies of God's coming judgement upon them (6:13–15). He proclaimed instead that the temple could only be the dwelling place of God if the people stopped oppressing the 'alien, the orphan, and the widow' and if they turned away from other gods (7:1–7). The prophets insisted that the temple was not a box which put

Yahweh in the possession of the people. It was the place of the promise of God's presence to his faithful people.

The judgement of which Jeremiah spoke came in the form of the Babylonian invasion, the destruction of the temple and the deportation to exile in Babylon. However, rather than being an end to the story of God's people, the exile became the beginning of a new phase in their history. Through the prophetic witness of Isaiah and Ezekiel they came to see the exile as a time of cleansing and refining through which God was preparing them for their restoration to the land and the rebuilding of their temple. The apparent failure of the present became the ground upon which the hope for the future was built. And the temple played a vital part in that hope. One day YHWH would return to his temple and all people would acknowledge him as Lord (Isa. 52:7–10; Isa. 60; Ezek. 37:28; Mal. 3:1–4,12). In the post-exilic period Zechariah and Malachi continued to centre the prophetic hope on the rebuilding of the temple and the coming of YHWH's saving presence to his people.

In one way it looked as if all this had happened by the time of Jesus. The people had returned from Babylon. Jerusalem had been rebuilt and the new temple, which had been completed during the reign of Herod the Great, covered a quarter of the city's surface area. Sacrifices and festivals abounded. Priests and high priests flourished. But all was not well. The land was occupied. Oppression and injustice prevailed. The temple did not appear to have been visited with the glorious return of YHWH's presence to Zion as was prophesied by Isaiah and Ezekiel (Isa. 52:8, Ezek. 37:26–8, 43:1–7). Hence, there was an ambivalence towards the second temple. On the one hand it was the everyday expression of Israel's monotheism embodying Israel's belief that the one God had chosen to dwell amongst them. It was sacred ground which would be protected at all costs from pagan influence. It became the focus of a great variety of cosmological and theological thinking. It came to be seen as the centre of the universe, a meeting place between heaven and earth and as one point at which the primal perfection of Eden – God resting with his creation – had been preserved. On the other hand it was clear that the fullness of God's presence – the eschatological presence of God – had not yet come, for on that day 'all the nations shall stream . . . to the mountain of the Lord, to the house of the God of Jacob' beating their weapons of war into instruments of peace and throwing away their idols as worthless trinkets (Isa. 2:2–4, 20; Mic. 4; Isa. 65). The day of God's dwelling amongst his people would be the day of salvation. Such a day had not yet come and so they still awaited the real return from exile and the coming of the real presence of God to dwell in their midst as the 'everlasting light' (Isa. 60:19–20).[15]

Christian use of the attributes, figures and temple of God

The essence of early Christian experience was that the promise had been fulfilled. The day of salvation had begun. God had revealed himself fully, acted decisively and had come to dwell amongst his people. As the early Christians tried to make sense of this experience they took the categories and ideas circulating in the Jewish world and applied them to Christ in radical ways. Jesus not only spoke the Wisdom and the Word of God, he embodied them. He was God's Wisdom and Word – the presence and action of God on earth. Jesus was not only the eschatological agent of God's kingdom, he exercised the Lordship of the kingdom which belonged only to God. Jesus not only brought people into the presence of God and enabled them to worship, he was the one in whom God was experienced and through whom worship was offered. Hence, they worshipped him. They knew that in Christ they were dealing with God, so they bowed down before him.

There is no denying that this was a definite turning-point in the development of Christian faith but it was not seen by those who took it as a denial of their Jewish monotheistic inheritance. Indeed, in Paul's teaching about how Christians should view food on sale in the market-place which had been previously offered to idols, he quotes the *Shema* – the critical monotheistic text – to make it clear that no other gods but the one God of Israel exist. He then goes on to reinforce his argument by repeating the *Shema*, although this time recasting it in a new light:

> for us there is one God, the Father, from whom are all things and for whom we exist, and one Lord Jesus Christ, through whom are all things and through whom we exist. (1 Cor. 8:6)

Paul's version of the *Shema* is highly instructive. On the one hand he sides firmly against the pagan duplication of divinity. Clearly then he did not believe that the place of Christ in Christian worship constituted a break with Jewish monotheism. On the other hand, by including Christ within the divinity of the one God he was offering a radical reinterpretation of monotheism. Although this theological reconstruction of the concept of God only came to formal and official expression in the creeds of the fourth century, the essential step had been already made. As Larry Hurtado argues in his study of early Christian devotion, 'in its crucial first stages, we have a significantly new but essentially internal development within the Jewish monotheistic tradition, a mutation within that species of religious devotion'.[16] Paul would have agreed and he would have said that the new direction was dictated not by the futile speculations of human reason but by the revelation of God:

> But we speak God's wisdom, secret and hidden, which

God decreed before the ages for our glory... these things God has revealed to us through the Spirit: for the Spirit searches everything, even the depths of God. (1 Cor. 2:7,10)

IV PERSPECTIVES: HEBREWS, JOHN AND REVELATION

Hebrews: the God of peace, the high priest and the eternal Spirit

In many ways the method of the writer of the letter to the Hebrews is very similar to the one I have adopted in this book.[17] The categories and experience of worship are used as the lens to explore a particular area of Christian doctrine in order to encourage the followers of Christ in their faith. The theological focus for Hebrews is the reality of salvation in Christ; the pastoral need is for Christians facing the pain of persecution to stand firm in their confession of Christ.

In order to define the significance of Christ the letter takes some of the familiar themes of Jewish thought about the relationship between God and the world, and then breaks new – and distinctively Christian – ground with them. It begins by demonstrating that Christ is qualitatively different from the angelic mediators of contemporary Jewish theology. Christ is the 'heir of all things', 'the reflection of God's glory and the exact imprint of God's very being' (1:3). He bears the name which is 'more excellent than theirs' (1:4) – the name of the Son. The proof of his absolute superiority is that he is worshipped by the angels (1:6) and accorded divine honour by the Father (1:8–9). Also in Hebrews 1 the wisdom and word motifs are brought into play to show that Christ is the one through whom God creates and speaks. But the themes are pushed beyond their previous limits. Christ is not simply an *instrument* through whom God is acting or an *idiom* for personifying the activity of God but an *identity* in whom the wisdom and the word – the creative and revealing work of God, together with his redemptive action (1:3) – are embodied. Similarly in chapter 3 Hebrews likens Christ to Moses but then clearly distinguishes them, first by underlining their different relationship to God (Moses was a servant, Jesus is a son), and then by comparing the effectiveness of their ministries (Christ leads the people of God into the true promised land – the longed-for sabbath of God's rest with all creation and, unlike Moses, he is not defeated by their sin). The difference between them is again summed up in language drawn from the world of worship: 'Jesus is worthy of more glory than Moses' (3:3). Despite Moses' significance he remains only a *brick* in the house of God. Jesus belongs to God, the *builder* of the house, and therefore shares intrinsically in his glory.

This Christological and doxological attention to the status of Christ should not distract us from the overriding thrust of the book which is about how Christ leads us into the holy presence of God. The framework of the letter is a comparison between Jewish liturgical practices and Christian experience of worship. Hebrews takes the imagery of the temple and the sacrificial ministry of its priests and describes them as a shadow of the reality which has come in Christ. The letter argues that the sacrificial system could not deal effectively with the problem of human sin because it left the fabric of the worshippers' moral lives untouched. The temple ritual of priest and sacrifice left them unable to bear the holy presence of God. The promise of human perfection and of participation in the presence of God was still awaiting fulfilment (11:39–40). Besides, the temple was made only with human hands (9:11) and therefore ultimately had to be distinguished from rather than equated with the real presence of God. Jesus, however, is the *perfect priest.* As the Son he represents God to humanity and as our brother he represents humanity to God. And he offers the *perfect sacrifice.* In his self-giving movement of obedience to

God he gives himself over to the judgement of God for the forgiving of others. In so doing he proves that humanity has been re-formed in his own person into the perfection God desires and requires. As the pioneer and perfecter of our faith he ascends into the *perfect temple* – the eschatological reality of the actual presence of God. He has become not merely the agent or means of our salvation but 'the source of our salvation' (5:9). By participating in his life through faith and baptism we too are taken into the uncreated tent of God's holy presence to worship him with 'reverence and awe' (9:11, 12:28).

Hebrews implores its readers, who are clearly tired and worn down by the pressures of persecution, 'to enter the sanctuary by the blood of Jesus, by the new and living way that he has opened for us through the curtain, that is through his flesh' (10:19–20). The writer is not just referring to a mental attitude or spiritual state but to the concrete action of taking part in the worship of the Christian community – and probably alluding to the Eucharist itself. The letter tells the people that as they confess Christ in their worship so they experience the reality of eschatological salvation: they stand in the reality of God's holy presence. As a result of such an encounter they will be strengthened to confess Christ through their witness in the world.

Hebrews therefore sees our worship taking place before the presence of God, in and through the priestly mediation of Christ our high priest. But what does it say about the Spirit? It has to be admitted that on the surface it says very little. However, the few references it does make are highly significant. First, the Spirit is seen as the witnessing Spirit who speaks through the Scriptures about Christ (3:7, 9:8). Second, the Spirit is the eschatological Spirit who comes to us with the life of the world to come (6:4). As the perfection which has been achieved by and in Christ is the eschatological salvation into which we are invited, it seems reasonable to assume that Hebrews envisages our participation in the ascended Christ takes place by the Spirit who comes amongst us with 'the powers of the age to come' (6:5). Third, Hebrews describes Christ offering himself to God 'through the eternal Spirit' (9:14). This is within a sentence which seeks to assure us that the blood of Christ will 'purify our consciences from dead works to worship the living God'. Christ is the priest who, by becoming the victim, offered the sacrifice for sin once for all. This work is done. But as the priest of the eternal order he continues to pray for his people and to offer their praise, perfected in his, to the Father; he is 'a minister [*leitourgos*] in the sanctuary', or leader of our worship (8:1). Now if the way Christ offered himself to the Father on the cross was by the Spirit, we can safely assume that the way he goes on offering our worship to the Father is by the same Spirit. So we have here an indication that Christian worship does not just take place *in* God's presence but, in some sense, *within* God's presence, for we are taken into the dynamic between the Father, the Son he begets as his exact image and the Spirit who exists eternally.

John: Father, Son and Spirit

John's Gospel provides enough material for several books on the trinitarian experience of God.[18] I want to home in on chapter 14 where John deals with the apparent problem of the imminent departure of Jesus. The chapter is full of liturgical significance. It faces the question of how Jesus' followers relate to God after his death and resurrection. The setting is the Last Supper in which Jesus washes his disciples' feet and warns them of his coming betrayal and death. Chapter 13 ends with Jesus saying to Peter: 'Where I am going, you cannot follow me now, but you will follow me afterwards' (v. 36). Chapter 14 begins with Jesus explaining that he is going to his death *alone* in order that he might go *ahead*. He is going through death to his 'Father's house' to prepare a place for them so that 'where he is, they may be also' (vv. 2–3). Near the beginning of the Gospel Jesus had described the temple as his 'Father's house' and then referred to his own body as the temple which, if destroyed, would be raised up in three days (2:16–19). Now in chapter 14 the theme of the temple once again becomes prominent. Jesus is to pass through death to enter the place of the Father's presence. But he goes before the disciples not just as one who blazes the trail to God's presence but as the one who is himself *the way* in whom and through whom they step into the temple, the sacred space of God's presence.

John goes on to justify such a claim by describing the relationship between Jesus and the Father (vv. 5–13) and then the relationship which Christians have with Jesus because of Jesus' relationship with the Spirit and their experience of the Spirit (vv. 15–26). It is as if John is delicately opening a precious gift before our eyes, unwrapping each interconnected and overlapping piece of paper at a time. He is like someone baking an exotic cake, gently folding in one ingredient after another; or like a painter carefully building up the various layers of colour until the richest image emerges. Jesus is able to bring the disciples into the Father's presence because he is 'in the Father and the Father is in' him (v. 10). To know Jesus is to know the Father, to see Jesus is to see the Father, to pray in Jesus' name brings glory to the Father.

Although the disciples find it difficult to understand what Jesus means by the interpenetration of Son and Father he assures them that when the Spirit comes they will know the reality of the mutual indwelling of Father and Son in the depths of their experience, because the relationship between Father and Son will be the source of their new life (vv. 19–20). Jesus says that he will not leave them as *orphans* but will come to them. Westcott's classic commentary on John says of Jesus' description of the disciples as orphans, 'the very word which describes their sorrow also confirms their sonship'.[19] Jesus promises the disciples, 'those who love me will be loved by my Father, and I will love them and reveal myself to them' (v. 21). In Jesus they will be where Jesus is, caught up into the filial relation, raised into the heavenly place, for as Westcott again puts it, 'heaven is where God is seen as our Father'.[20] Hence the full recognition of Jesus' true identity (as the only Son of the Father) and the corresponding recognition of their true identity (as children of the Father) will not be for the disciples merely a matter of intellectual awareness or cerebral assent, it will be a deep and life-changing experience that comes through the indwelling of the Spirit whom Jesus and the Father send. The Spirit will come to the disciples with all the personal characteristics of one who teaches and reminds and who can be received or rejected. The Spirit is distinct from the Father and the Son – another, not the same counsellor. The Spirit brings us into the presence of Christ, the Father's home where fullness of life is to be found and true worship given (see 4:20–4). A very popular post-communion prayer draws on the imagery of Luke's story of the lost son but it also captures something of the pattern of the gift which John unfolds:

> Father of all,
> we give you thanks and praise,
> that when we were still far off
> you met us in your Son and brought us home.[21]

The chapter ends where it began, with comfort in the face of death: 'Do not let your hearts be troubled' (v. 27). Jesus says that the time for talking is passing and the time for dying is drawing near. He has to demonstrate to the 'ruler of the world' that he does well what we fail to do – he does 'as the Father commands'. Jesus obeys not out of fear or because of any need for self-justification but simply because he loves the Father (v. 31). This love, exposed and proved by death, will conquer the world, and by the Spirit the followers of Jesus will be drawn into this love which the Son has for the Father as they see, even share in, his glory (see 17:22,24). 'Rise', says Jesus, 'let us be on *our way*' (v. 31).

Revelation: the one who sits on the throne, the Lamb and the seven Spirits

The Revelation or Apocalypse (the Greek for *uncovering*) of John is not laced with the clear trinitarian references to Father, Son and Spirit such as which we find in the Gospel of John and which we detected in one form or another in the Pauline literature and in Hebrews. Nevertheless it has a highly sophisticated doctrine of God which is deeply and richly trinitarian. As with everything else in the book, Revelation's understanding of God is expressed in a strange and complex array of symbols and images and so can remain hidden and obscure. We are so distanced from the apocalyptic tradition of writing which Christians inherited from Jews, with its invitation to see earth with the eyes of heaven, and so remote from the political context to which the apocalyptic writings were addressed, that the book of Revelation often remains a foreign and distant text. The lens of worship helps us to get the book into focus because John uses liturgical categories, most notably the distinction between true and false worship, as his main theological tools.[22] But before concentrating on the way he wields these tools, I want briefly to mention two other areas which are of interest for our exploration of the trinitarian experience of God in the life of the New Testament Church: John's experience of God through his vision and the relationship between Revelation and the worship of the communities to which it was written.

JOHN'S VISIONARY EXPERIENCE

The way in which John received the Revelation was explicitly trinitarian. When he was 'in the Spirit on the Lord's Day' (1:10) he saw a dazzling vision of the figure of Christ who then unfolded the revelation which had been previously entrusted to him (1:1). While he was worshipping in the Spirit, he encountered the person of Christ and was then taken before the presence of God to see things as they really are. Hence the revelation came from God, was communicated by the word of Christ and was received through the activity of the Spirit.

THE RELATIONSHIP BETWEEN REVELATION AND THE WORSHIP
OF THE EARLY CHRISTIAN COMMUNITIES

Revelation clearly has close associations with the worshipping life of the churches to which it was written.[23] Like other New Testament documents it would have been publicly read in the worship of the churches – taking about an hour and a half to read from beginning to end. Indeed, it begins with a strong admonition for this to happen and it ends by drawing the listeners into the familiar cry of the Church: 'Amen. Come, Lord Jesus' (22:20). With its concentration on the decisive significance of the death of the Lamb, its vision of the marriage supper of the Lamb and his bride and its concluding yearning of the Spirit for the completion of God's purposes, Revelation would have been ideally appropriate for the early Christian communities to read as they gathered in the Eucharist to proclaim the Lord's death until he comes.

The number of hymns quoted, the many liturgical sounding phrases used, the allusions to baptism and the Eucharist, the emphasis on prophecy through the power of the Spirit and the vivid scenes of worship pictured, all suggest the echoes of the worship of the early Church which resound throughout the book. This is important for our purposes because the worship of heaven which Revelation describes most certainly involves the worship of Jesus and relates the Spirit to the person of Christ and the presence of God in the closest way. John introduces and summarizes his imagery in his opening greeting:

> Grace to you and peace from him who is and who was and who is to come, and from the seven spirits who are before his throne, and from Jesus Christ, the faithful witness, the firstborn of the dead, and the ruler of the kings of the earth.
>
> To him who loves us and freed us from our sins by his blood, and made us to be a kingdom, priests serving his God and Father, to him be glory and dominion for ever and ever. Amen. (1:4–6)

God is the one 'who is and who was and who is to come'. The Spirit, drawing upon the imagery of Zechariah's vision (Zech. 4:1–14), is the seven spirits who surround God's throne. Jesus is the 'faithful witness' who by his death and resurrection forms us into a priestly people to serve his God and Father – and for so doing is given glory.

REVELATION'S USE OF WORSHIP AS A THEOLOGICAL TOOL

Revelation is uncompromisingly monotheistic in the strict Jewish sense of commanding that worship can be given only to God. The 'eternal gospel' (14:6) proclaimed by the angel is its central message:

> Fear God and give him glory, for the hour of judgement has come; and worship him who made heaven and earth, the sea and the springs of water. (14:7)

The historical situation faced by the churches was that the world was worshipping the beast and tempting them to do the same (13:3–4). The Roman Emperor had been exalted to divine status. His image – busts of his face – was found on the street corners and demanded homage (13:11–18).

Pagan rites tattooed demonic symbols onto people's skins and Roman documents with their imperial stamps pressed them into the service of the Empire's commercial and social structures. A war was being waged for the allegiance of the peoples of the earth – including the members of the Church (13:11–18) – by the threefold deceit of the dragon (ch.12), the beast to whom he gave authority (13:1–10) and the second beast who beguiles the world. The impending judgement of which Revelation warns will be directed at those who, showing no signs of repentance, worship the beast and its image and are marked with his sign (14:9–10, 16:2,9). The criterion for salvation will be simply whether people have remained faithful to 'the testimony of Jesus' and worshipped God alone (20:4).

Revelation uses a device common in Jewish and Christian apocalyptic writings to underline that only God may be worshipped. On two occasions (19:9–10, 22:8–9) John is so overwhelmed by all he sees that he falls down to worship the angel who shows him the vision of heaven. Both times the angel rebukes him and commands him to worship God (the source of the revelation) not 'a fellow servant' (the messenger of salvation). In the first scene he is told that 'the testimony of Jesus' and the 'spirit of prophecy' (19:10) demand worship of the one God alone. Hence, Jesus is seen as the one who in life and in death stood against any form of idolatry and the injustice and oppression which inevitably follows in its wake. He bore the faithful witness to the one God and his kingdom of righteousness. Prophecy which is truly inspired by the Spirit will exhort Christian communities to stand in solidarity with Christ, maintaining his faithful witness, even to the point of death. By so doing they will not only gain their own salvation but will also present a compelling witness to the nations. Their witness will bring the truth about God, counteracting the deceit of the beast and so enabling the conversion of the nations away from

the idolatrous pretensions of the beast to the cause of Christ
– the worship of the one God and the coming of his
kingdom (15:2–4). There can be only one object of worship
because there can only be one creator. No matter how
powerful the beast may appear, he is only part of the created
order. God is the source of all things – the Alpha and
Omega. Everything else is dependent upon God. The
acknowledgement of this dependence is the beginning of
worship. It is the sign of a right relationship between the
people and the basis of the right ordering of human life.
Denial of it is the beginning of idolatry and signals the
usurpation of finite ambitions into the realm of the ultimate
and self-existent. The testimony of Jesus, maintained in the
Spirit-led life of the Church, is that only God is the Lord, all
other claims to *ultimate* authority, whether religious,
political, economic or social, are to be rejected.

In the light of this radical Jewish emphasis on the
supremacy of the one God, it is remarkable but highly
significant that Revelation allows Jesus to be worshipped
and bestows titles and functions on him which belong only
to God (1:17, 7:10, 17:14, 22:13). In chapters 4–5 the door
of heaven is opened and John, in the Spirit, sees the divine
presence – pictured as a throne 'with one seated upon it'
(4:2) – surrounded by the heavenly beings worshipping the
one God. As the vision develops John sees a 'Lamb standing
as if it had been slaughtered' (5:6) move towards the throne
to take the scroll 'from the right hand of the one who sat
upon it' (5:7). At this the heavenly creatures fall before the
Lamb, the prayers of the saints rise before him and the 'new
song' of worship to him begins: 'You are worthy...'
(5:9–10). Then the living creatures are joined by the
myriads of angels 'singing with full voice: "Worthy is
the Lamb..." ' (5:11–12). Finally the whole of creation
joins them in singing:

'To the one seated on the throne and to the Lamb
be blessing and honour and glory and might
for ever and ever!' (5:13)

Notice both how calculated Revelation is in allowing the Lamb to be worshipped and how careful it is to ensure that there remains only one object of worship. Worship of the Lamb is not in addition to the worship of the one God, it is included within the worship of the one God. The Lamb is not on another throne. He is at the centre of the throne (7:17). In one of his several detailed studies of the book of Revelation, Richard Bauckham writes:

> Since the issue of monotheistic worship is so clear in Revelation, it cannot be that the worship of Jesus is represented in Revelation through neglect of this issue. It seems rather that the worship of Jesus must be understood as indicating the inclusion of Jesus in the being of the one God defined by monotheistic worship.[24]

This is the critical point. The book of Revelation – which claims to uncover the hidden things of God – considers that the Lamb who suffered to defeat evil belongs to the very being of God. The transcendence of God does not distance him from the world but gives God freedom to enter his creation, participate in its pain and conquer its sin. This is why all creation joins in the new song giving blessing, glory and might to the Lamb (5:13), for in the Lamb, the Lord has come.

As well as including the Lamb within the one divine reality symbolized by the throne, John also includes the seven spirits (signifying the Spirit of God) within the being of God. John's imagery is drawn from Zechariah's vision (Zech. 4:1–14) in which he saw a golden lampstand with seven shining lamps representing 'the eyes of the Lord which range through the whole earth' (Zech. 4:10). They are

God's Spirit by which he will accomplish his purposes (Zech. 4:6). John pictures God's Spirit in the form of seven lamps burning before the throne thereby both associating the Spirit with the presence of God and yet, differentiating the Spirit from the one who sits on the throne. Revelation also intrinsically relates the seven spirits to the Lamb. The eyes of the Lord in Zechariah's vision effecting God's will on earth become in John's vision the eyes and the horns of the Lamb 'sent out into all the earth' (5:6). They represent God's power in all its fullness at work in the world to bring about the victory gained by the death of the Lamb.

The work of the Spirit includes his prophetic ministry within the Christian community encouraging the followers of Christ to maintain their witness and to await eagerly the eschatological completion of God's plan of salvation. In 21:10 John is carried by the Spirit to see 'the bride, the wife of the Lamb' (20:9). Already he has glimpsed their marriage feast and seen the bride clothed with the fine linen of her 'righteous deeds' (19:6–9). Now he is given a vision of the marriage home, the new Jerusalem where God dwells with his people and calls them his children. Unlike Jewish eschatological visions there is no temple in Revelation's new Jerusalem 'for its temple is the Lord God and the Lamb' (21:22). Here the servants of God will 'see his face' (22:4).

The link between the eschatological experience of salvation of the new Jerusalem and the present reality of the Church's life as it battles with the forces of Babylon is the 'new song' which the Church sings as it worships God as revealed in Jesus Christ. Even now the Church is a kingdom of priests giving glory to the Father and the Son by the power of the Spirit. Even now it bathes in the living waters of baptism (22:17) and tastes the eucharistic bread of heaven (3:20, 19:9). And even now the Spirit forms the features of the eschatological Church into the Church of the present by inviting her to echo the Spirit's longing for the completion of God's purposes by crying 'Come, Lord Jesus' (22:17).

The Spirit's role is to create a future in which God will be seen 'face to face'. By a skilful use of the categories of monotheistic worship Revelation unveils the reality of the one God to reveal the threefold identity of the one who sits on the throne, the Lamb standing in the centre of the throne and the Spirit surrounding the throne. This is a fitting place to end our study of worship in the New Testament. For Revelation claims that Christian worship has a trinitarian pattern precisely because the one God exists in a trinitarian way.

4

ooooooooo

The Worship of the Evolving Church

Over all we receive we bless
the Maker of all things through his Son
and through the Holy Spirit.
Justin Martyr (c. 100–65)[1]

I FROM THE NEW TESTAMENT TO THE MIDDLE OF THE SECOND CENTURY

Setting the scene

It would be wrong to give the impression of a clear break between the life of the Church in the New Testament period and in the decades which followed. Many of the characteristics of the New Testament Church continued. The Church was still young and growing rapidly. The uneasy relationship with Judaism and the Roman Empire persisted and, indeed, deteriorated. An anathema directed against Christians and other supposedly heretical groups had been introduced into Jewish worship making it impossible for Christians to share in the life of the synagogue. The threat of Roman persecution had now become a grim reality and the cost of the Christian discipleship could be calculated in the blood of the martyrs. The writings of Paul, Luke, John and others were circulating and gaining an implicit authority, though they were still some way off being formed into that which we know as the New Testament, with its canonical status.

Liturgical principles and texts were evolving but still little was fixed and formalized.

The main writers providing evidence about the life of the Church for this period are known as the *Apostolic Fathers.* Their writings are in the same genre as many of the New Testament documents. They are letters from leaders of the Church to different Christian communities seeking to deepen the faith of the believers and to encourage them in the way of Christ. They differ by not having quite the same sense of creative innovation found in the New Testament or the sense of creative application found in the theologians of the latter part of the second century and in the third. They were people who knew they held within their hands a pearl of great price but they did not attempt to analyse its fundamental structures or to discern its many patterns. They simply described the treasure, so that those who had discovered it could live within its riches and those who were still searching for it would be attracted by the beauty of its truth.

Christian worship in the pagan world

Christian faith was a confusing phenomenon for its pagan observers. On the one hand it claimed to be monotheistic in the tradition of the Jewish faith. On the other hand, it gave divine status to the human figure of Jesus. As far as the political philosophy of Rome was concerned, it combined the worst of both worlds. Its adherence to monotheism meant that it refused to give ultimate allegiance to the emperor and to take part in the sacrificial religious practices towards the Roman deities which were believed to be religiously necessary for the maintenance of the society's life. Its adherence to Jesus and its worship of him appeared to present a perverted form of monotheism which had neither the intellectual appeal of pure Jewish faith nor,

because of its exclusive character, the practical advantages
of pagan polytheism. Celsus, the second-century opponent
of Christianity, complained that: 'If these men worshipped
no other God but one, perhaps they would have had a valid
argument against the others. But in fact they worship to an
extravagant degree this man who appeared recently, and yet
think it is not inconsistent with monotheism if they also
worship his servant.'[2]

The perception of Christianity was that it combined a
religious concentration on the person of Jesus with a continuing commitment to the exclusive principles of Jewish
monotheism. The various apocryphal Acts of the Apostles
show how this basic pattern, which we have discerned in the
New Testament, was the driving dynamic of the Church's
missionary activity. Although not actually written until
towards the end of the second century and beginning of
the third, the apocryphal Acts, with their unreflective and
somewhat crude theology, have the same feel as the writings
of the earlier period and so help us to see how conversion
to Christianity was represented in popular preaching
throughout the second century. In short they depict the
adoption of Christian faith as a matter of turning from
idolatry to the worship of the one God who is known and
honoured and worshipped in the person of Jesus. Worship
of other gods is to be abandoned in favour of worship of
Jesus. But the worship of Christ is not another form
of idolatry. It is the form in which the worship of the one
God is to be truly found; for in and through Christ, by the
work of his Spirit, God the Father is to be encountered.

Examples of pastoral ministry from the period give a
similar, though more carefully presented, picture. An
anonymous sermon from the early second century put it in
this way: 'We ought to think of Jesus Christ as we do of God
– as the "judge of the living and the dead". And we ought
not to belittle our salvation. For when we belittle him, we

hope to get but little.'[3] The nature of Christian salvation leads the believer to 'think of Jesus Christ as of God'. But as the sermon goes on to say, such devotion is to be completely distinguished from pagan sacrifices to 'dead gods', for through the living Christ believers 'come to know the Father of Truth'.

This conviction that Christ is the one by whom God has saved us and through whom we worship God, is clearly expressed in the letter of Clement of Rome to the Corinthian Church at the end of the first century. Clement repeatedly refers to Christ as the Saviour through whom we enter the presence of God and through whom we glorify God. He also frequently refers to the Spirit, most notably in terms of the Spirit inspiring the Scriptures, including the writings of Paul. When exhorting the Corinthians to unity, he appeals to the trinitarian basis of their faith: 'Do we not have one God, one Christ, one Spirit of grace which was poured upon us?'[4]

Ignatius (*c.* 35–*c.* 107), Bishop of Antioch, wrote in a similar vein to the Ephesian Christians. He appealed for unity and likened Christians gathered in worship around their bishop to a choir singing 'in unison and with one voice to the Father through Jesus Christ'.[5] In the same letter he described the trinitarian character of Christian life and worship with another analogy: 'Like stones of God's temple, ready for a building of God the Father, you are being hoisted up by Jesus Christ, as with a crane (that's the cross!), while the rope is the Holy Spirit. Your faith is what lifts you up, while love is the way you ascend to God.'[6] For Ignatius the Church is truly the dwelling place of God because through faith its members are joined to Christ (whom Ignatius calls 'our God'[7]) and by the work of the Spirit, they are filled with a divine love.

The trinitarian pattern of Christian existence to which Ignatius appealed was most clearly shown in the baptismal practice of the first- and second-century Christians and was also given regular expression in the Eucharist, which he encouraged the Ephesians to celebrate more frequently. There will be more to say about both in the next section. At this stage it is sufficient to mention the Didache, a manual of Church discipline which, at least in its liturgical parts, gives every impression of containing early material. It instructs that baptism should take place 'in the name of the Father, Son and Holy Spirit'.[8] By the end of the first century baptism in the threefold name was the standard practice of the Church. Thanksgiving in the Eucharist is to be given to the Father for all he has 'revealed through Jesus' and Christ is invoked.[9] The Spirit is not explicitly mentioned but we must remember the early Christian belief that all worship by definition takes place in the Spirit. Interestingly the Didache envisages occasions when prophets will preside at the Eucharist and says that the Church 'should let them give thanks in their own way'. Later it refers to them speaking in the Spirit, showing how the Spirit's general presence within the community as it worshipped and the Spirit's inspiration of particular moments in worship was seen as intrinsic to the nature of worship.

Finally, the martyrdom of Christians provides another source for early Christian attitudes to worship. We have already seen that Roman persecution of Christianity had its roots in the refusal of Christians to participate in the cult of the emperor and in the worship of Roman deities. It was this which led to their martyrdom, for such an offence was punishable by death. Several accounts of martyrdom show how the martyrs both refused to swear the religious oath to the emperor (on the grounds that they worshipped only the one God) *and* affirmed the divinity of Christ. Possibly the oldest and probably the most moving account is of the martyrdom of Polycarp. Polycarp (*c.* 69–155) was Bishop of Smyrna, a town to the north of Ephesus on the western edge of modern day Turkey. Around the middle of the second century a period of persecution arose against the Smyrnian Church. Its bishop was one of the victims. During his interrogation he was asked, 'What harm is there to say, "Lord Caesar", and to offer incense and all that sort of thing to save yourself?'[10] For Polycarp there was great harm in doing so. Later, in the arena, the proconsul insisted, 'Take the oath, I shall release you. Curse Christ.' Polycarp replied, 'Eighty-six years I have served him, and he never did me any wrong. How can I blaspheme my King who saved me?' We are told that the crowds shouted with 'uncontrollable anger and a great cry': 'This is the ... father of Christians, the destroyer of our gods, who teaches many not to sacrifice or to worship'.[11] As he was tied to the stake Polycarp prayed his final prayer:

> Lord God Almighty, Father of your beloved and blessed Servant Jesus Christ, through whom we have received full knowledge of you, 'the God of angels and powers and all creation' and of the whole race of the righteous who live in your presence ... For this and for everything I praise you, I bless you, I glorify you, through the eternal and heavenly High Priest, Jesus Christ, your beloved Servant, through whom be glory to you with him and Holy Spirit both now and to the ages to come. Amen.[12]

It is quite likely that parts of the account have been influenced by later hagiography and that its theology, particularly the concluding doxology of Polycarp's prayer, has been neatened by later orthodoxy, but the main lines of the account ring true historically. It is significant that in the account of Ignatius's martyrdom, his final prayer is also distinctly trinitarian.

Polycarp, Ignatius and their brothers and sisters in martyrdom had been baptized in the name of the Father and the Son and the Holy Spirit, they had lived their Christian lives in service to Christ, by the work of the Spirit for the glory of God. Now, as they gave up their lives for this faith, they prayed in the only way they knew how: to God, through Christ, in the Spirit.

II FROM THE MIDDLE OF THE SECOND CENTURY TO THE END OF THE THIRD

Setting the scene

It is always somewhat artificial to divide up historical periods. In many ways the Church continued a very similar existence throughout the second century and into the third. It was still very much a missionary movement expanding numerically and geographically. It still faced many places and periods of persecution as well as safer environments and times. The New Testament documents still had not been formally fixed into the scriptural canon as we know it, although most had gained a recognized authority and were treated as inspired Scripture. Worship still had not arrived at anything like a prescribed liturgical form and both the free and fixed continued to live together, with great local variety. Nevertheless, by about the middle of the second century it had become clear that the Church faced two particular challenges.

The first was to attempt to answer the sort of questions people like Celsus, mentioned earlier, were raising. As the Church took root in the great cities of the ancient world, the claims of Christian faith came into increasing contact with the philosophical and theological assumptions of a culture dominated largely by Greek thought. A collection of Christian thinkers and writers emerged who attempted to give a reasoned explanation of Christian faith, correcting misunderstandings and commending Christian faith in language accessible to the educated world. They have become known as the *Apologists*. The second challenge concerned the integrity of the Church's own life and thought. As the Church worked towards a mature understanding of its claims to truth it had to sift out those theological positions which, in the long term, were inconsistent with its fundamental convictions. The developing understanding of the Church's trinitarian experience of God in salvation and worship always played a critical part in both the process of self-understanding and the apologetic task. So before considering specific examples of the liturgical life of the Church, it is worth pausing to make some general comments about the main features of Christian experience that emerge from the period.

At the grassroots level of ordinary Christian life Christ was experienced as the revealer and saviour. He was believed to reveal God as God truly is. He was known to bring salvation by enabling people to know God and to be known by God. The Spirit was experienced as the Spirit of prophecy, the bringer of truth, the one who inspired the Jewish Scriptures and the Christian apostles and the one who continued to speak through the Church's prophets to lead the Church into a fuller grasp of Christ's revelation and salvation. The Spirit was the one who related the believer to Christ and, through this union, sanctified both the individual and the community. This work of Christ and of the Spirit was seen as nothing less than the work of God.

The twin themes of the Christian experience of salvation, the Spirit and Christ, formed the structure of Christian worship. Documents from the early third century describing contemporary worship tell us that the worshipping community is the 'place where the Holy Spirit abounds',[13] for 'prayer is . . . said through the Holy Spirit, and the eucharist is accepted and sanctified by the Holy Spirit, and the scriptures are the words of the Holy Spirit'.[14] Worshippers gathered in the Spirit, in the name of Christ. They met on the first day of the week, the new day, the day of the resurrection, to celebrate their salvation in Christ, to receive Christ as the bread of life, to confess Christ as Lord, to hear his teaching, to pray through him and to seek to live his life. Usually they risked ridicule, such as the third-century graffito which depicted someone in prayer before a cruci-fied man with the head of a donkey and the inscription, 'Alexamos worships his God'. Sometimes they faced vio-lence and death. There were many to follow in the footsteps of Ignatius and Polycarp as the decades unfolded. Why? What caused them to adopt this new religion of the crucified Jew? It was because by the Spirit and through Christ they knew they had entered into a saving relationship with God. As we unpick some of the particular features of their worship we must not lose sight of this energy and movement which lay at its heart.

Baptism

Justin Martyr (*c.* 100–65) was one of the Apologists. In a carefully written defence of Christian faith addressed to the emperor, he explained how people are admitted to the faith: 'Those who are persuaded and believe that the things we say are true and promise that they can live accordingly . . . are then washed in the water in the name of God the Father and Maker of all, and of our Saviour Jesus Christ, and of the Holy Spirit.'[15] It was dramatically done. Confession of the Father was followed by a first immersion, confession of the Son by a second and confession of the Spirit, by a third.

Irenaeus (*c.* 115–90), Bishop of Lyon, in his *Demonstration of the Apostolic Preaching*, provides a summary of the bap-tismal teaching which the candidates had to affirm before they could be accepted for baptism.

This is the rule of our faith, the foundation of the building and what gives support to our behaviour.

God the Father uncreated, who is uncontained, invisible, one God, creator of the universe; this is the first article of our faith. And the second is this:

The *Word of God*, the Son of God, our Lord Jesus Christ, who appeared to the prophets according to their way of prophesying, and according to the dispensation of the Father. Through him all things were created. Furthermore, in the fulness of time, in order to gather all things to himself, he became a human being amongst human beings, capable of being seen and touched, to destroy death, bring life, and restore fellowship between God and humanity. And the third article is:

The *Holy Spirit*, through whom the prophets prophesied, and our forebears learned of God and the righteous were led in the paths of justice, and who, in the fulness of time, was poured out in a new way on our human nature in order to renew humanity throughout the entire world in the sight of God.[16]

It has been suggested that the baptismal formula forced theology in a trinitarian direction. Once people had been baptized in the name of the Trinity and taught to pray in a trinitarian way, the Church's theology had no choice but to justify its practice and to reconcile it with belief in the one God. But baptism in the threefold name was more than a liturgical formula. Irenaeus shows that it was the articulation of the Christian understanding of salvation. Christian baptism took place in the name of the Trinity because the Christian faith into which people were baptized had a trinitarian shape.

Irenaeus spent much of his energy trying to counter the pervasive heresy of Gnosticism. Gnosticism (from the Greek word *gnōsis*, meaning knowledge) was a hybrid form of religion – a sort of half-baked Christianity in which many of the aspirations and concepts of Christianity coalesced with the assumptions and categories of contemporary pagan religious movements. The result of this unnatural alliance was that, using Irenaeus' analogy, the foundations of Christian faith were undermined. Gnosticism effectively denied the Christian understanding of the creation of the world by God, the activity of God in the world through Christ by the Spirit and the salvation by God of the created order, including the renewal of human life.

In his *Against the Heresies* Irenaeus insisted that the rule of faith – the trinitarian summary of belief affirmed at baptism – *is* the confession of the Church. Writing from France, probably the furthest western edge of the Church's expansion, Irenaeus declared that this is the essence of Christian faith which is believed throughout the Church.[17] Irenaeus' first concern was for the truth. He argued passionately that God had revealed the truth about himself. The history of salvation, including the creation itself, is the story of God revealing his identity. The Church's task is to 'lay hold of the tradition of the truth'[18] which it has received from the Apostles. Only this brings the truth of God's relation to us and our relation to him and therefore only this brings life.

The identity of God revealed by the story of salvation is trinitarian. The story of creation is the story of the saving action of God. Gnosticism assumed that the creation was the work of an inferior being acting independently and, as sometimes conceived, disobediently to God. Irenaeus contended that the creation was the work of God's 'own self' through his Word and Spirit, God's two hands. The Word and the Spirit belong eternally to God but for the purposes of creation and salvation they are expressed. Always implicit within God they became explicit. In language which became part and parcel of the Church's trinitarian vocabulary, Irenaeus said that the Son is both coexistent with the Father and generated by him. Irenaeus believed that this generation, or expression of an integral dimension of his nature, happened at a particular point for a particular purpose.

The history of the people of Israel is the story of God relating to his people by his Word and his Spirit. Through his Word God appears to Abraham at the oaks of Mamre and speaks to Moses from the burning bush. By his Spirit God anoints the leaders of Israel and prophesies through Isaiah and Ezekiel. The story of Christ is the story of God's Word becoming incarnate through the work of the Spirit, for Jesus is 'truly human and truly God'.[19] This great sweep of salvation history becomes a personal story of salvation when we enter the waters of baptism, by which 'God bestows on us regeneration through his Son by the Holy Spirit'.[20]

Through the work of the Spirit we are drawn into the life of Christ to participate in his life of love with the Father. The identity of God revealed through salvation history, affirmed in the baptismal faith, experienced in Christian life, was most clearly expressed, as far as Irenaeus was concerned, in Ephesians 4:6 which states that there is 'one God and Father of all, who is above all and through all and in all': 'For *over all* is the Father and *through all* is the Son, for through Him all things were made by the Father, and *in all* is the Spirit, who cries Abba Father, and fashions us into the likeness of God.'[21]

From Irenaeus, a bishop in France, we turn to Tertullian (*c.* 155–220), the son of an African centurion. After a fairly stormy youth he was converted to Christianity and became a brilliant theologian leaving a lasting impression on trinitarian theology. His writing on the Trinity is mainly found in his *Against Praxaeus.* Tertullian believed that Praxaeus had been instrumental in undermining the Church's confidence in the prophecies of Montanus, the charismatic leader whose sect Tertullian was eventually to join. In *Against*

Praxaeus Tertullian was concerned mostly with Praxaeus' denial of any distinction between the Father and the Son but he saw Praxaeus' neglect of the distinct activity of the Spirit as the other side of the same coin. Praxaeus believed the one God was capable of assuming different guises and that in Christ he had become incarnate and had been crucified. Like Irenaeus Tertullian argued from the story of creation and salvation that the Word and the Spirit, or as he preferred, God's Reason and Wisdom, belong eternally to the being of God. For the purposes of creation and salvation God has given voice to his Reason and expression to his Wisdom. Therefore the one God in his economy, or ordering of himself to create and to relate to that which is not God, is trinity. Tertullian liked to create new words and to use existing words in new ways. He felt this was demanded by the radical nature of Christian theology which is directed by God's definition of himself and is not controlled by existing human categories. In fact the very word 'trinity' (Latin, *trinitas*) was even invented by him and he was the first to talk of God as one substance in three persons.

What is most interesting about Tertullian is the way he argued that Praxaeus' notion of an undifferentiated unity of God failed to express the true character of Christian experience of God. It is not that we experience different modes or forms of the presence of the one God first, for example, as Father, then as Son and then as Spirit, but that we experience God's distinctions. It is not that we know God as Father, Son and Spirit in some sort of consecutive way but that we know God as Father, Son and Spirit simultaneously. Tertullian shows how our experience of God is the experience of the Son relating to the Father rather than simply the completeness of God relating to us as Son. He rooted his thinking scripturally by referring to various texts which he claimed reveal a dialogue between Father, Son and Spirit and by referring to Jesus' way of praying: 'He himself prays to the Father. When Peter recognises Him as the Christ he does not deny it . . . he rejoices in the Spirit and says to the Father, *I thank you, Father, that you have hidden these things from the wise*.[22] Christians affirm 'the plurality of the Trinity' because they are 'disciples of the Paraclete'[23] and have been initiated into the inner relatedness of God. Hence, Tertullian invited baptismal candidates to call upon the Father and the Son to give the Spirit so that they may enter into the fullness of Christian existence.

Origen (*c.* 185–*c.* 254), another North African, grew up in Alexandria, a city steeped in Greek culture which became a great centre of Christian theology. He too was extremely influential on trinitarian theology. We shall meet more of his thought in the next section but it is important to make two points about his theology here. First, he affirmed the trinitarian pattern of the baptismal life and its theological implications in a way similar to Irenaeus and Tertullian. He showed how we are brought to a knowledge and love of the Father through the revelation of the Son by the work of the Spirit. Quoting 1 Corinthians 2:10 Origen explained how the Spirit is the one who searches out the deep things of God and is therefore the one through whom Christ reveals the Father and the one by whom we participate in the life of Christ. Second, he successfully moved the understanding of the Trinity beyond the thought of Irenaeus and Tertullian by maintaining that the Son's generation from the Father is an eternal act. The Son's generation is not a product of God's relation with the creation but an eternal happening in the life of God. Likewise the Spirit proceeds from the Father as an eternal feature of the Father's nature. Origen thus conceived of God's being as an eternal event in which the Father generates the Son and breathes the Spirit. This development in trinitarian theology is of critical significance to the understanding of baptism because it grounds the pattern of salvation in the

101

pattern of God's eternal being. It assures us that God is trinitarian towards us because God is trinitarian in his eternal reality. The way we know God in salvation and worship is the way God is in his eternal life.

Prayer

The practice of calling upon the name of Christ in prayer as a source of help, healing and salvation which we saw amongst the New Testament communities continued into the second and third centuries in much the same way. Irenaeus, for example, insisted that 'invocation of the name of Jesus Christ' is the principle of 'separation and division' amongst the peoples. Only the name of Christ can save and only those who call upon the name of Christ are saved. He explained how believers who have found salvation in Christ will naturally invoke him in prayer and that 'he is near and present, fulfilling the requests of those who with pure hearts call upon him'.[24] Clearly the name of Christ was found to be effective in ministry and worship. Irenaeus tells how exorcisms, healings and even the raising of the dead took place in the name of Jesus and how people received words of knowledge, vision, prophecy and a multitude of other gifts through the name of Christ.[25] Christians prayed to the Father in the name of Christ and were equipped with the gifts of the Spirit for the ministry and worship of the Church.

Irenaeus knew that all this could play right into the hands of the Gnostics. Gnosticism in its various forms invoked human, angelic and semi-divine intermediaries which it believed filled the space between God and the creation. In its Christian form it simply slotted Christ into this hierarchy. Although Christ was placed at the top of the scheme, he was still ultimately distanced from the pure reality of God. As well as denying the true divinity of Christ, Gnosticism also denied his real humanity. Christ did not actually become incarnate, he only appeared to do so. It was a strictly dualistic system in which the spiritual and the material could have no real relationship. Irenaeus overcame the problem of the apparent separation between God and humanity with his doctrine of creation and incarnation. God's Word, by which he created all things, became incarnate in Christ and 'conversed with his own creation'.[26] Prayer is the reply. Conversation with God is in the name of Christ because Christ is God's mode of communication with his people.

The *Apostolic Tradition of Hippolytus* shows how the pattern of prayer arising from the practicalities of Christian ministry and worship became ordered in the liturgical prayers of the Church. The *Apostolic Tradition* is a third-century Church Order giving instructions about various liturgical matters. Its prayers have a clear trinitarian structure. The prayer of ordination is typical:

> God and Father of our Lord Jesus Christ, Father of mercies and God of all comfort . . . Pour out now your power of your royal Spirit, which you gave to your beloved Servant Jesus Christ, which he bestowed on his holy apostles . . .

The prayer concludes with a doxology:

> Through your Servant Jesus Christ our Lord, though whom be glory, might and honour to you, with the Holy Spirit in your holy church, both now and always and world without end. Amen.[27]

Earlier we saw how Tertullian identified the trinitarian character of Christ's own prayer. This led him to see Christian prayer as something new and distinctive. It is not just a particular example of the human instinct to pray. It has been forged in the praying of Christ and therefore has a divine character. He encouraged people when praying not only to lift their hands in the traditional style of prayer but to spread them wide to signify Christ and his cross and to declare thereby that Christian prayer takes place because of Christ and through Christ and in Christ. Prayer, for Tertullian, also takes place *to* Christ in the sense that as the Son of the Father he is inseparable from the Father. Because God is only known as Father through the Son, Tertullian considered it natural for Christian prayer to be orientated to both. As he was at pains to point out to Praxaeus, this does not blur the distinction between Father and Son, it simply shows that the divinity of God cannot be conceived apart from the Son.[28]

Origen was of a different mind concerning prayer to Christ. He argued that prayer and worship should be offered only to the Father. He appealed to Scripture. The Lord's Prayer shows that Jesus taught us to pray to his Father 'with and through him'[29] and Paul describes how the Spirit joins us with the prayer of Christ to cry 'Abba Father'. Origen was quite clear that prayer could not be offered apart from Christ. It is only through the Son that we can know God and relate to the Father. Christ is therefore our high priest through whom our prayer and praise are offered and our brother into whose filial relationship we are adopted. But he argued that to offer prayer to Christ disturbs the delicate balance of the Christian doctrine of God on a spiritual and theological level. The essence of the spiritual life is union with Christ through the activity of the Spirit. As we are made more fully perfect by the sanctifying work of the Spirit so we receive Christ more deeply and know his Father more truly. In this way we are drawn by the Spirit into the Son's eternal contemplation of the Father.

Origen's theological reservations about prayer to Christ became more precise in the Dialogue with Heraclides. Heraclides was a bishop whose orthodoxy was under question. Origen had been called in by Heraclides' church to establish whether the charges were fair. During his interrogation he sought to clarify whether Heraclides believed in the full deity of Christ *and* in his distinction from the Father. To this end he even required Heraclides to admit that there are 'two Gods'. In the next breath Origen went on to explain that although Christian faith asserts the deity of Christ it does not conflate Christ with the Father. The Christian concept of divinity includes both Father and Son. However, although it distinguishes between Father and Son it does not separate them. Christ is not a competing divine figure with the Father. Origen then appealed to the pattern of Christian prayer to prove that it protects Christian faith from any implication of polytheism: 'Offering is universally made to Almighty God through Jesus Christ inasmuch as, in respect of his deity, he is akin to the Father. Let there be no double offering, but an offering to God through God.'[30]

There are not two objects of worship. There cannot be two ultimate sources. Hence, the Church, in its universal practice, does not make 'a double offering'. It worships only God. But it does so through the Son, who shares the Father's deity. The Church's worship is divine worship both in the sense of being offered to the one divine source alone, and in the sense of being a participation in the worship taking place within that divine life. It is likely that Heraclides' church addressed its eucharistic prayers to the Son. Origen urged the adoption of the customary practice of directing prayer to the Father in order to avoid unnecessary theological confusion.

Origen's reluctance to offer worship directly to Christ, however, cannot be explained entirely in terms of him seeking to preserve the trinitarian geography of Scripture which is orientated towards the Father. It had deeper roots in his underlying view of reality. Origen's great strength was his ability to communicate Christian faith in ways which made sense within the contemporary philosophical world. But this was also his weakness. He was so influenced by the current form of Platonism, which provided the intellectual backdrop to the thought of his time, that he carried through too many of its basic assumptions into his understanding of God and his dealings with the creation. Mid-Platonism (as it was called) was so committed to the principle of protecting the pure being of God from the material world of becoming, with its change and decay, that it envisaged a series of divine emanations from God, each possessing an inferior degree of divinity. This is why Origen was prepared to call the Son 'Second God' (corresponding to mid-Platonism's *Logos*) and why he could conceive of the Spirit as 'Third God' (corresponding to mid-Platonism's World-Soul). Origen believed that prayer to Christ was not just inadvisable. It was not permissible. Christ is not God in the absolutely pure sense in which the Father is God. He is not, therefore, the object of our worship and religious attention.[31]

Eucharist

Although we may have an example of a eucharistic prayer addressed to Christ in the East Syrian liturgy of Addai and Mari,[32] most of the evidence we have about the Eucharist in the second and third centuries supports Origen's claim that eucharistic prayers were addressed to the Father. Justin tells us that 'over all we receive we bless the Maker of all things through his Son Jesus Christ and through the Holy Spirit'.[33] The *Apostolic Tradition* provides us with the oldest surviving example of a complete eucharistic prayer:

> We render thanks to you, O God, through your beloved child Jesus Christ, whom in the last times you sent to us as saviour and redeemer and angel of your will;
> who is your inseparable Word through whom you made all things, and in whom you were well pleased . . .

106

After giving thanks for the birth, life and death of Christ
and rehearsing Jesus' words at the Last Supper, it continues:

> Remembering therefore his death and resurrection, we offer
> to you the bread and the cup, giving you thanks because you
> have held us worthy to stand in your presence and minister
> to you.
>
> And we ask that you would send your Holy Spirit upon the
> offering of your holy Church; that, gathering them into one,
> you would grant to all who partake of the holy things the
> fullness of the Holy Spirit for the confirmation of faith in
> truth.
>
> That we may praise and glorify you through your child Jesus
> Christ, through whom be glory and honour to you, to the
> Father and the Son and the Holy Spirit, in your holy Church,
> both now and to the ages of ages. Amen.[34]

In the Eucharist Christians celebrated the saving action
of God in Christ and rejoiced that they had been welcomed
into the reality of God's presence.[35] They prayed for the
fullness of the Spirit's work. They received Christ as the
bread from heaven. The Eucharist was seen as the fulfilment
of Malachi's prophecy that God's name would be glorified
among the Gentiles and a pure offering would be made
to him among the nations (Mal. 1:10–11).[36] This was an
important text for Irenaeus who believed that the Eucharist
represented the anticipation of the Christ's eschatological
renewal of all creation. The first fruits of the new, transformed creation are offered to God in the purity of praise
and the divine name the Father has shared with the Son is
glorified in the Church across the nations.[37]

III THE FOURTH CENTURY

Setting the Scene

The fourth century was a period of massive change for the Church. Fiercely persecuted at the beginning of the century under the Emperor Diocletian, it had become the state religion of the Roman empire by 324 under Constantine. The ramifications for worship were enormous. New freedoms and new converts led to the building of great basilicas, the creation of new liturgies and the development of extended processes of initiation. Ecclesiastical organization, with its tendency towards clericalization, increased, the monastic movement, with its rigorous aesthetic and liturgical demands, grew, and pilgrimages became a popular feature in the piety of the wealthy.

The most important issue for the worship of the Church concerned the theological disputes which raged throughout the century on the nature of the God Christians worship. The time had come to give precise and consistent formulation to its central claims. As Richard Hanson puts it, 'From the beginning Christianity carried within its bosom two convictions: that there is only one God and that Jesus is divine ... These two convictions had to be reconciled'.[38] Earlier and incomplete attempts to reconcile the two had been made but now the Church was forced to provide a definitive, credal expression of its faith in God.

The Council of Nicea

Origen detonated the explosive conditions of the theological dispute. Arius (*c.* 250–336), an Alexandrian presbyter born in Libya, lit the fuse. Despite Origen's exceptional knowledge of Scripture and his deep sensitivity to the nature of Christian prayer and worship, he was guilty of superimposing the image of the gospel onto an alien philosophical framework. His diffused understanding of divinity with its perceived need to protect the pure being of God from direct contact with the creation by a series of buffers with decreasing degrees of divinity, exposed fundamental fault lines in the Church's use of the *Logos* doctrine from at least the time of Justin, and caused a resurgence of the proper concerns of Jewish monotheism.

Arius and his supporters wanted to return to the biblical world-view which made a clear divide between God and the creation. In 318 he took the brave step of publicly criticizing the Christological teaching of his bishop, Alexander (Bishop of Alexandria). Arius insisted that Christ did not belong to the divinity of God. He is, like us, part of the created order. He is the highest of all creatures but still a creature and, therefore, ultimately 'alien and dissimilar in all respects to the Father's substance and individual being'. Contradicting Origen, he claimed that 'there was a time when [the Son or *Logos*] was not'.[39] The *Logos* had been created by God in order to be the principle through which God would create and relate to all else. The *Logos* had become incarnate in Christ but this was not the incarnation of God because the *Logos* was not God. Nevertheless, in our relationship with God he functions as God because he is all we know of God.

The Council of Nicea was called in 325 by the Emperor Constantine to settle the fierce debate that ensued and to bring peace to the Church and stability to the Empire. The bishops sided against Arius and declared that Christ is 'of one being [*homoousios*] with the Father'.[40] Like Arius they were concerned to protect the unity and integrity of God by drawing a sharp line between the Creator and the creation. Unlike Arius they placed Christ firmly on the side of God. However, the creed they issued did not end the matter. In fact it led to a cauldron of theological controversy made even more complex by political manoeuvring in the state as

well as the Church. Some Church leaders effectively sought
to revoke, or at least reinterpret, the Nicene decision, while
others aimed to justify its position and clarify its terminology.

Athanasius

Athanasius (*c.* 296–377), Bishop Alexander's successor,
became the leading defender of Nicene theology.[41] As well
as arguing for the divinity of Christ against the Arians he
also found himself using very similar arguments for the
divinity of the Spirit against the 'Tropici' – Athanasius' name
for a movement later in the century which recognized the
Son as divine but which reduced the Spirit to the level of a
creature. By focusing on Athanasius we will be able to
identify many of the themes which united the orthodox
theologians of the fourth century as they sought to express
the trinitarian faith.

Athanasius held faith and godliness (devotion or piety)
in the closest possible relationship. Faith is the Church's
response to the God who has addressed and encountered
us in Christ. It is the obedient acceptance of God's self-
interpretation, the grateful confession of God as God has
shown himself to be. Godliness (*theosebeia* or *eusebeia*) is, in
the words of Thomas Torrance, 'an embodiment of faith . . .
in a corresponding way of life and worship in the service of
God'.[42] Athanasius maintained that the belief in the divinity
of the Son and the Spirit is enshrined in the tradition of the
Church and can be received only by a 'godly and reverent
mode of reason'.[43] Such an attitude of mind and way of life
is formed by conscious and committed participation in the
worshipping life of the Church. It is a case of allowing
the full implications of Christian worship, as it responds
to the trinitarian revelation of God, to become the criteria
for discerning the truth. Arius' scheme failed primarily

because it denied the convictions implicit in the nature of Christian worship. For Athanasius the character of worship was defined by Jesus himself when he told the Samaritan woman that 'true worshippers will worship the Father in spirit and truth' (John 4:23): 'True worshippers, therefore, worship the Father, but in Spirit and Truth, confessing the Son and in him the Spirit. For the Spirit is inseparable from the Son, as the Son is inseparable from the Father.' Athanasius went on to say that we should, 'after the pattern of true worshippers, confess and side with the truth'.[44] In other words, Christian theology is bound by those consistent realities in the worshipping life of the Church which, in their turn, have been formed by the action of God on his people and continue to be sustained by the relationship of God's own self with his people. Three of these realities stand out clearly in Athanasius' writings.

The first is the worship of Christ. If Arianism was right then the Church's worship was blasphemous. It was worshipping a creature rather than the Creator. Athanasius argued that Christ is adored precisely because he is 'the Son of the adorable Father' and not part of the created order. Just as light belongs intrinsically to the sun, so Christ belongs essentially to the Father. Hence, 'we adore, confessing Him as Lord and God, because we are creatures and other than he'.[45]

The second follows on directly. Arius' denial of the divinity of Christ negated the fundamental conviction of Christian faith and worship that through Christ we relate to God and God relates to us as *Father*. Athanasius argued that the scriptural word for God is Father. He pointed to Jesus' command to call God 'our Father' in prayer and to baptize 'in the name of the Father, and the Son and the Holy Spirit'.[46] If Arius was right, Athanasius contended, and the Father does not eternally have a Son, then God is not eternally (intrinsically or essentially) Father – God became a

Father when he created the Son to create all else through him. Therefore, our faith does not tell us the truth about God and our worship does not worship God as God truly is. The true identity and reality of God lie behind the one we know as the God and Father of our Lord Jesus Christ. Indeed, if Christ does not share being with God then Christ cannot reveal God to us because, by Arius's own admission, Christ, like us, is distanced from God by the divide between the Creator and his creation. In that case, our worship is destined always to miss the target because it is not focussed on the true being of God.

Further, unless the Father is truly the Father who eternally generates the Son, there is no basis or ground within God's being for God's action of creating us to be his children and, correspondingly, no mode of relationship within the being of God into which we can enter by baptism. Peter Widdecombe defines Athanasius' understanding of God in this way: 'The Father in Athanasius' theology is the word that identifies God's being as fruitful, inherently generative, relational, and dynamic; it is the word that indicates that the divine being exists first as the relation of Father and Son.'[47] Athanasius maintained that the eternal generosity of movement in which the Father generates the Son and the eternal relationship between them means that our adoption as God's children in baptism and our conversation with God through prayer is a real participation in the true life of God. Without such movement and differentiation God is deficient in power (for he needs something other than himself in order to create) and neutered in love (for he is not *by nature* personal and relational, generous and loving).[48] Athanasius sought to establish (against the Arians) that the Son is proper to the Father's being and (against the Tropici) that the Spirit is proper to the Son's being and therefore also to the Father's. Father, Son and Spirit are

112

inseparably related and their life of love is the basis of our lives of love with God and with each other.[49]

The third feature of worship prominent in Athanasius' defence of Nicene theology is the action of baptism in the threefold name.[50] Of course both Arians and Tropici would have used the threefold formula and, in most cases, used a threefold immersion. Athanasius showed that they denied its implications. His argument was simple. Baptism signifies the gift of salvation. Salvation involves being united to God. If Christ is not divine, he cannot unite us to God, for he too is distanced from God. Similarly, if Christ's divinity is accepted but the Spirit's denied, the same problem remains. The Spirit can only unite us to the divine Son if the Spirit too is divine. Baptism (which by the fourth century would have included a post-baptismal sealing or confirming in the Spirit) is the sacrament of our salvation because we are given to participate in the Spirit and, by the Spirit (who is one with the Son) we are united to Christ, and through Christ (who is one with the Father), we are brought into saving relation with the Father and so share in the life of God. Refusal to acknowledge the divinity of the Son and the Spirit reduces baptism to a meaningless rite and the hope of salvation to an illusionary dream.

The Cappadocian Fathers

Basil of Caesarea (*c.* 330–79), his brother Gregory of Nyssa (*c.* 330–95) and their friend Gregory of Nazianzus (330–89) were Church leaders in Cappadocia, the eastern side of modern day Turkey. They had a decisive influence on trinitarian theology. By the time they came to prominence the debate about the divinity of the Son had been largely settled in Nicea's favour. The focus had shifted to the question of the divinity of the Spirit and to the problem of properly distinguishing between Father, Son and Spirit so as to avoid them simply becoming different names for the one divinity. I will concentrate on Basil because his arguments are explicitly based on the realities of Christian worship.

Basil was a liturgist. His liturgical work represents an important marker in the process of liturgical development. As with other periods in the life of the early Church, it is dangerous to generalize about worship in the fourth century. In many ways the liturgy depended on where you were – in Egypt or Jerusalem, West or East Syria, Asia Minor or West Europe. It could also depend on the nature of the Christian community with its particular theological affiliation, and certainly on the style of the liturgical leaders who were still allowed to adapt texts and extemporize prayers. Nevertheless, as Basil himself admits, the most typical form of prayer and praise was directed *to* the Father, *through* the Son *in* the Spirit. Textual evidence is not difficult to find.[51] It is the pattern in the *Sacramentary of Serapion* from Thmuis in Egypt in the middle of the century and in the *Apostolic Constitutions* from Antioch in West Syria towards its later stages. It was the natural form of Christian prayer, reflecting the pattern of Scripture and the structure of spirituality. We have seen examples of it throughout this chapter. Although the *Apostolic Tradition* from Rome in the third century includes the Holy Spirit in ascriptions of praise, the evidence suggests that as the fourth century progressed, Christ and the Spirit became more self-consciously included as objects of the doxology in addition to being the means by which praise was made. In other words, rather than glory being given to the Father, through the Son, in the Spirit, it was offered to the Father *together with* the Son and the Spirit. We can see this in the *Canons of Hippolytus* and in the earliest examples of the *Liturgy of St Mark*, both of which came from Egypt in the late fourth century, and in the *Testament of our Lord* from Asia Minor towards the end of the century.

Basil clearly played a deliberate part in this process. He

was accused of introducing a new doxology giving glory to the Father and the Son *with* (or *and*) the Holy Spirit.[52] His handiwork can be seen in his own eucharistic prayer from which the *Liturgy of St James* is derived, used today in the Orthodox churches on certain occasions. Although he claimed traditional precedent for its form he recognized that there was something new in his attempt to secure its mainline usage. His reasons for improving the liturgy were the same as his reasons for wanting to add to the creed defined at Nicea in 325.[53] The creed and the liturgy should give voice to the baptismal faith of the Church. He argued that his doxology articulated the full implications of Christian faith and worship:

> For myself, I pray that with this confession I may depart hence to the Lord, and them [those accusing him of unnecessary innovation] I charge to preserve the faith secure until the day of Christ, and to keep the Spirit undivided from the Father and the Son, preserving, both in the confession of faith and in the doxology, the doctrine taught them at their baptism.[54]

The baptismal faith is rooted in Christ's command to baptize in which 'he conjoined'[55] the Spirit to the Father and himself. The Spirit thus brings us into fellowship with the Son and his Father because the Spirit has fellowship with them both, being as intrinsic to the life of God as our spirits are to us. Hence Basil said: 'We have deemed ourselves under a necessary obligation to combine in our confession of faith him who is numbered with them at baptism, and we have treated the confession of faith as the origin and parent of doxology.'[56] Of course Basil had no theological problems with the older form of doxology. It expressed the dynamic of the Christian experience. Our relatedness to God is through Christ and *in* the Spirit. This is how God comes to us and how we come to God. But he insisted that glory must be also directly ascribed to the Spirit *with* the Son and the Father because the Spirit shares with them the same glory.

Basil's claim for the full divinity of the Spirit was anchored in the baptismal faith but it stretched to include the whole history of salvation and the continuing characteristics of Christian life and worship. By the Spirit God created. Through the Spirit God spoke. In the Spirit God worked through the life of Christ. By the Spirit God raised Christ from the dead and will renew the face of the earth. The Spirit is the activator of mission and ministry, evoking faith in Christ, bringing healing and equipping the saints with the gifts for Christian living. The Spirit is the enabler of worship, bringing forgiveness of sins, speaking through prophecy and Scripture and ordering the life of the Church. Because the Spirit is the one who makes us holy and gives us knowledge of the Father and the Son – both of which are necessary for us to become worshippers of God – Basil told his readers, 'If you remain outside the Spirit you will not be able to worship at all'.[57] In this way he turned the argument of his opponents on its head. They maintained that because we worship *in* the Spirit, the Spirit cannot be divine – for the Spirit is not worshipped. Basil showed that it is precisely because we do worship in the Spirit that the Spirit must be divine – for it is only through God's own Spirit that we can truly know the reality of God and really enter into his presence.

Basil, like the two Gregories, had a strong sense of the distinct identities of Father, Son and Spirit, each of equal honour and due equal glory. We conclude by looking at how the Cappadocians sought to safeguard the unity of the one God. Their argument at each point was related to the reality of worship.

First they recognized the *mystery of God's unity.* God's oneness is three-dimensional: 'the Godhead is . . . undivided in separate persons'[58] (as Gregory of Nazianzus put it) . Gregory explored Scripture's analogy of light and suggested that Father, Son and Spirit equal 'Light thrice repeated; but one Light and one God.' He went on to provide a concise definition of the Trinity in this way: we see 'Light (the Son) out of Light (the Father) in Light (the Holy Spirit)'.[59] Like the other Cappadocians he knew the demands such ideas put on our language and understanding. His advice was not to expect to *comprehend* the mystery of God but to allow oneself to *apprehend* the reality of God in the worshipping life of the Church as it responds to God's own self-definition and self-giving: 'This, then, is my position and that of whosoever is dear to me, to worship God the Father, God the Son and God the Holy Spirit: three persons, one Godhead, undivided in honour and glory and substance and kingdom.'[60]

Second, the Cappadocians saw the activity of Father, Son and Holy Spirit as three interpenetrating moments of *one divine life and will*. Gregory of Nyssa made much of this when defending Cappadocian thought against the charge of tritheism: 'every operation which extends from God to the creation . . . has its origin from the Father, and proceeds through the Son and is perfected in the Holy Spirit.'[61] This differentiated understanding of the saving movement of the one God was the basis of their theology of baptism. The Father adopts us into his life through the person of the Son by the activity of the Spirit. This is one movement of love by the one Godhead.

The third way in which the Cappadocians secured the unity of God was by emphasizing the *monarchy, or sole source, of the Father.* Although the Son and the Spirit are fully divine, their divinity is founded upon the divinity of the Father by whom the Son is eternally generated (or begotten) and from whom the Spirit eternally proceeds (through the Son, as Gregory of Nyssa would add). The order of this eternal

117

action is reflected in the direction of Christian prayer. We pray to the Father through the Son in the Spirit.

The final way in which they safeguarded the unity of God was by clarifying the language of trinitarian theology. The Synod of Alexandria in 362 had agreed to talk of one *ousia*, three *hypostaseis* but this was to cause some confusion because in the Greek of the time *ousia* and *hypostasis* could both mean 'being'. The Cappadocians tightened the terminology by referring *ousia* to the being of God and *hypostasis* to the particular way, mode or manner by which the being of God is expressed. The one God is God in three ways of being God. Father, Son and Spirit all possess the common nature of God but are distinguished by their 'expressed particularities',[62] their different identities. The critical contribution of the Cappadocians was to show that the identifying characteristics of the hypostaseis is *their relation to the others.*[63] Hence, although each is God, each also implies the other. This means that the one being of God cannot be conceived of except in terms of the mutual relatedness of Father, Son and Spirit for it is their life of love which constitutes the one being of God. The contemporary orthodox theologian, John Zizioulas, uses the elegant phrase 'being as communion' to describe the Cappadocian concept of God.[64] The reformed theologian Colin Gunton builds upon Zizioulas' interpretation and maintains that Cappadocian thought was a 'theological revolution' because it was:

> a revolution in the way in which the word *God* was to be understood. God *is* no more than what Father, Son and Spirit give to and receive from each other in the inseparable communion that is the outcome of their love. Communion is the *meaning* of the word: there is no 'being' of God other than this dynamic of persons in relation.[65]

Participation in the relatedness of God is the joy of Christian

118

worship. By giving glory to the Father and the Son and the Holy Spirit we share in the eternal giving and receiving of life and love which constitutes the very being of God.

The Council of Constantinople

The full divinity of the Son had been defined at Nicea in 325 and enshrined in its creed. In 381 the full divinity of the Spirit was defined at Constantinople and the following clause was added to Nicea's simple 'we believe in the Holy Spirit':

> the Lord, the giver of life,
> who proceeds from the Father,
> who with the Father and the Son is worshipped and
> glorified,
> who has spoken through the prophets.[66]

Although none of the bishops of the western Church were in attendance, the Nicene-Constantinopolitan Creed gained ecumenical acceptance and found its way into eucharistic worship, where it remains. Later trinitarian theology, including the great work of Augustine in the next century, and later liturgical life were no more than attempts to explore and celebrate the faith of the Church defined at Constantinople that the one God is eternally Father, Son and Spirit. As Athanasius said, this is the perfection of theological truth and 'the true and only divine worship'.[67]

PART TWO

STRUCTURE
ooooooooooo

5

∞∞∞∞∞∞∞

The Glory of God

'Lord, I have sought thy face;
thy face, Lord, will I seek.'
(St Anselm)

In Part One we examined the origins of the doctrine of the Trinity in the worshipping life of the Early Church. In Part Two we turn from this historical approach to a more thematic analysis in order to probe more deeply into the structure of the doctrine. As we said at the beginning of the book the aim of these chapters is to take concepts and categories which arise from the sphere of worship and use them as lenses through which to view the Trinity or, to change the analogy, as keys to unlock our understanding of the doctrine.

It is worth reminding ourselves of why this is a good way of doing trinitarian theology. First, as we have seen in Part One, the essence of the doctrine of the Trinity was first articulated in worship. Furthermore, during the whole process of the formulation of the doctrine, worship acted as a custodian of the trinitarian revelation of God and as a criterion for judging whether theological statements remained faithful to the way God had shown himself to be. Second, worship is therefore 'The School of the Trinity'. It is the means by which we respond to the God who has revealed himself through Christ and in the Spirit. It is where

123

we meet with God and learn from God. It is where God impresses himself upon us. Third, the realities of worship are the common stuff of Christian life. Simply by worshipping God as Christian believers the fundamental structures of trinitarian theology are erected in our minds, hearts and spirits. We are on home ground when we look at the Trinity from the perspective of worship. We do not approach it as amateurs. We come as professionals – people who are already practitioners of the doctrine in our daily lives. We come as speakers to God who are seeking to speak about him more confidently. And we come as people who have been spoken to by God and who are ready to listen to the sound of his voice more clearly.

I THE GLORY OF GOD

Defining the terms

When King David brought the ark of the covenant to Jerusalem there were extravagant scenes of worship. The air was filled with the sound of harps, symbols, drums and shouts of joy and David was 'dancing before the Lord with all his might' (2 Sam. 6:13). When the ark was placed in the Tent of Meeting a huge number of fellowship offerings were made, enough we are told for the roasted meat to be shared out among every man and woman in Israel. And why should there not have been such an explosion of emotion? After all, the ark was not simply a symbol of national identity. It was the glorious presence of YHWH. The origins of Psalm 24 may well lie in this highly charged arrival of the ark in Jerusalem.

> The earth is the Lord's and all that is in it,
>   the world, and those who live in it;
> for he has founded it on the seas,
>   and established it on the rivers.

Who shall ascend the hill of the Lord?
>And who shall stand in his holy place?

Those who have clean hands and pure hearts,
>who do not lift up their souls to what is false,
>and do not swear deceitfully.

They will receive blessing from the Lord,
>and vindication from the God of their salvation.

Such is the company of those who seek him,
>who seek the face of the God of Jacob.

Lift up your heads, O gates!
>And be lifted up, O ancient doors!
>That the King of glory may come in.

Who is the King of glory?
>The Lord, strong and mighty,
>the Lord, mighty in battle.

Lift up your heads, O gates!
>and be lifted up, O ancient doors!
>that the King of glory may come in.

Who is this King of glory?
>The Lord of hosts,
>he is the King of glory.

The psalm probably reached its final form after Solomon's temple had been built when it would have been developed and refined through its use in an annual festival in which the ark was carried in procession around the city and then returned to the temple.

The central concern of the psalm is the identity of both God *and* his true worshippers. It celebrates the three structures of the Jewish understanding of God. God is the creator who has fashioned the whole cosmos; the redeemer who has defeated all that sets itself against his purposes; the indweller, who resides with his people and makes them holy. It also handles three liturgical themes which run throughout the biblical narratives. The first concerns the holiness which God requires from the worshipper. Only those who have 'clean hands' (blameless conduct) and 'pure hearts' (right motives) and who have not lifted up their 'souls to what is false' (avoided idolatry) can enter into the presence of God and receive his blessing. In the next chapter we shall explore how God both demands and supplies holiness in the worshipper. At this point all we need to note is that Hebrew religion held together the ritual (the way we worship) and the moral (the way we live) together in a proper understanding of God. When YHWH, the God of Israel, is identified as the one divine creator, redeemer and indweller, this God and this God alone should be worshipped and the way of this God, and his way alone, followed. Any attempt to separate worship from lifestyle, religion from ethics, the rites of the sanctuary from the life of the society was alien to the Hebrew understanding of its God and his calling upon them.

This chapter will focus on the two other major liturgical themes to be found in the psalm. The first of these is 'seeking the *face* of the God of Jacob'. The Hebrew word for 'face' is *panim*. It is the most common word used in the Old Testament to signify God's presence. Language about 'seeking God's face' had its origins in the royal courts of the ancient world where subjects would seek an audience with the king or ruler. To seek God's face meant to search, hope, long for a meeting, an encounter with YHWH. It was the desire to enter into God's presence *directly* and is expressed frequently throughout the psalms:

'Come,' my heart says, 'seek his face!'
Your face, Lord, do I seek.
Do not hide your face from me. (Ps. 27:8)

To say 'I am seeking God's face' became almost synonymous, as here in Psalm 27, with saying 'I am going to the temple'. The temple was seen as the dwelling place of God. It was the point at which God could be found; the place where God could be encountered.

The allusion to Jacob in Psalm 24 probably had its origin in the story of Jacob wrestling in the night with a mysterious figure and claiming in the morning that he had 'seen God face to face' (Gen. 32:30). For the Hebrews the face was a précis of the person. It was the mirror of the personality, expressing a person's true nature and revealing his or her intentions towards you. Jewish traditions believed that Jacob had in some way encountered the real presence of God and seen his true identity, though of course, talk of seeing God was also a highly risky, even dangerous business, as far as the Israelites were concerned. They knew that God is beyond our sight, for he is both immaterial and beyond our understanding. Because God is the transcendent creator, he cannot be controlled by our categories or grasped by our sight – even Jacob only saw the face of God in the darkness of the night.

The other liturgical theme I want to explore is closely related. It is the 'glory of God' which the psalm celebrates in its closing section. The Hebrew word for 'glory' is *kabod*. Its basic meaning referred to the impressiveness of a person signified by the greatness of riches (literally their weight), the gravitas of personality and the grandeur of status. It was the visible and tangible evidence of wealth, personality and power. *Kabod* also came to be applied to the impressiveness of God, or, more strictly, to the impression God's presence made on his people. The *kabod* of YHWH was the sensory impact of the invisible God. It was the effect of God's self-manifestation. It could be seen in thunder and lightning, fire and cloud. It was the display of God's power and strength, beauty and majesty.

As Psalm 24 shows, *kabod* became increasingly associated with the temple in Jerusalem. The psalm concludes with an entrance liturgy in which the worshippers, probably carrying the ark of the covenant, call upon the door-keepers to open the gates of the temple so that 'the King of glory may come in'. They are asked to say more about the one whose entry they are requesting. They reply by saying that God is the *king* whose glory is shown in his saving action in history as redeemer and through his cosmological control over all things as creator. This is the true identity of the one whose real presence comes to dwell in his temple to receive his people's praise. God's glory therefore is that which belongs to him by definition as creator and by demonstration as redeemer. It can be shared with no other (Isa. 42:8).

Glory is a fundamental theological concept – it speaks of the true nature of the one God. It is therefore a critical liturgical concept – only YHWH, the God of glory, can be given glory in worship. As with God's face so with God's glory, the Hebrews found themselves struggling with the tension between acknowledging their experience of the accessibility of God in their history and worship *and* maintaining their conviction of the distance of the God who refuses to be contained in human systems. Glory helped them to affirm both realities. On the one hand it was a description of God's transcendent qualities. On the other, it was a declaration of God's inexpressible splendour and beauty invading the present conditions of our world.

The glory of the face of God

The quest to see the face of God, to find out what God is like and to be admitted into his presence, belongs to the fundamental religious instinct of humankind. In her hit song *One of Us*[1] (which reached the British Top Ten in 1996), Joan Osborne asked:

> If God had a face
> What would it look like?

And would you want to see
if seeing meant that you
would have to believe in
things like heaven and in Jesus and the Saints
and all the prophets?

The restless quest of Osborne's song is also voiced in a well-known prayer based on some words of Augustine. This is a version familiar to Anglicans:

Almighty God,
you have made us for yourself,
and our hearts are restless till they find their rest in you:
pour your love into our hearts and draw us to yourself,
and so bring us at last to your heavenly city
where we shall see you face to face;
through Jesus Christ our Lord.[2]

The first half of the prayer derives from the first paragraph of Augustine's *Confessions*.[3] As the pages of his life story unfold we see the deep intellectual, physical, emotional and spiritual restlessness of Augustine leading him into all sorts of blind alleys before he is finally satisfied with the word of God in Christ. The second half of the prayer which speaks of the eschatological encounter with the face of God is like a summary of his great work *On the Trinity*, which begins and ends with a discussion of the heavenly vision when we shall be 'renewed by sight'[4] and see God face to face. We now live by faith, *trusting* that God truly is as he has revealed himself to be. We then move from faith to sight *knowing* that God really is as he has shown himself to be.[5]

An eighth-century English theologian, Alcuin of York, has left a lasting mark on English liturgy. He was heavily influenced by Augustine's thought. One of his collects echoes that sense of forward movement to the eschatological revelation of God and the transformation of humanity

which lay at the heart of Augustine's thought and was, as we
shall see, intrinsic to the biblical understanding of both the
face and the glory of God:

> Eternal Light, shine into our hearts;
> eternal Goodness, deliver us from evil;
> eternal Power, be our support;
> eternal Wisdom, scatter the darkness of our ignorance;
> eternal Pity, have mercy on us;
> that with all our heart and mind and strength
>   we may seek your face
> and be brought by your infinite mercy
>   to your holy presence;
> through Jesus Christ our Lord. Amen.[6]

Alcuin's and Augustine's sophisticated recognition that
in order to see the face of God we need to be first transformed into being capable and worthy of such a vision, had
its origins in the guts of Jewish religion. Hebrew faith knew
that the sight of God would be too much for humanity to
bear in its natural state. The remarkable thing about Jacob
was that he saw the face of God and survived. The story of
his struggle with the stranger in the night is a fascinating
one which weaves together his encounter with God and his
reconciliation with his brother Esau. Interestingly one of
the threads holding them together is the theme of the *face*.

Jacob is coming home. It is time to put things right with
his brother whose birthright he stole many years earlier. As
Jacob approaches Esau's estate with his entourage he sends
a gift ahead, thinking to himself: 'I may appease his *face* with
the present that goes before me, and afterward I will see his
face; and perhaps he will lift my *face*.'[7] But before he deals
with his brother, Jacob must deal with his God. The struggle
in the depth of the night is arrestingly depicted by Epstein in
a sculpture which stands near the entrance to the Tate
Gallery in London. Jacob is locked in combat with his

assailant, staring hard into the face and refusing to let go until the blessing comes. There is agony and intimacy, strength and tenderness, immediacy and distance. In the narrative Jacob demands to know the name of the one who has come so close. In Hebrew thought names of things and people reveal their character and nature. If Jacob could know the name of the divine assailant he would be able to categorize him and so have some control over him. The divine name is withheld, God will not be coerced. But the name of Jacob is changed. Jacob, meaning 'trickster' or 'supplanter', dies and Israel, meaning 'God preserves' or 'protects', is born. The abiding identity of the deity is revealed in the new identity of the person. God is a transforming presence.

'I have seen God *face* to *face*, and yet my life is preserved' (Gen. 32:30), says Jacob. Tantalizingly we are not told what Jacob actually saw. But if we stay with the narrative our curiosity is given some firm clues. The story goes from the meeting with God to the meeting with Esau. The passion of Esau's forgiveness and goodness is overwhelming. Esau runs to his brother, embraces him, falls on him and kisses him. They both weep. Their reconciliation cannot be bought with Jacob's gifts. It is given and given joyfully by Esau's grace. Jacob can only say, 'Truly to see your *face* is like seeing the face of God – since you have received me with such favour.' Earlier Jacob had prayed to the God of 'steadfast love and faithfulness'. Then, in the darkness of the night, he encountered the personal reality of this God and now, in the light of the morning, he saw the same goodness reflected in the compassion of his brother.

Stories about Moses are rich in the themes of the face and the glory of God and also, like the Jacob story, involve the name of God. Particularly interesting is Moses' dialogue with YHWH in Exodus 33:12–34:9. He is seeking reassurance that God's presence will remain with his people as they journey to the promised land. Not content simply with the promise of God's presence Moses asks YHWH to prove his presence by revealing his glory. The reply is both yes and no. God will manifest his presence and declare his nature but he will not allow Moses to see his face, 'for no one shall see [YHWH] and live' (33:20). In the scene of awesome proportions which follows, Moses is treated to the tender touch of God. He is placed in a cleft of a rock on Mount Sinai and then covered with the hand of God to shield him from the brilliance of the coming glory. As promised, God's presence appears and passes by Moses, proclaiming the name and nature of God: 'The Lord passed before him, and proclaimed, "The Lord, the Lord, a God merciful and gracious, slow to anger, and abounding in steadfast love and faithfulness" ' (34:6). God's face may have been hidden from Moses and Moses may have been protected from the full impact of God's glory, but he was assured, as Jacob had been before him, of the reality of God's presence and the identity of God's nature. The God who abides with his people is beyond any *material depiction*: he is YHWH, meaning 'the one who is and always is'. He simply exists. But this God can be defined by *moral description*. He is the God of steadfast love and faithfulness, full of grace and mercy, rich in forgiveness and committed to justice. To this God Moses bows down in worship and prays for his people.

The theme of the glory of God is prominent in the traditions about the Tent of Meeting and the temple. The most vivid example of the former is found in Leviticus 9. Moses had recently anointed Aaron as priest. He now instructs him to offer sacrifices in the tent so that 'the glory of the Lord may appear' (v. 6). After the sacrifices have been completed God's glory was indeed manifested 'to all the people' (v. 23). Fire consumes the offerings on the altar and the worshippers 'shout and fall on their faces' (v. 24). The dedication of Solomon's temple (1 Kings 8–9 and 2 Chron. 5–7) has similar features. During a spectacular liturgy with singers, musicians and priests all extolling the 'steadfast love' of God, the temple is filled with God's glory in such a tangible and sensory way that the priests are forced to the floor.

The account in 2 Chronicles includes a second manifestation of God's glory which is so overpowering that the priests cannot enter the temple and so overwhelming that all the people fall to the ground and worship God. In between the two appearances, Solomon prays. It is a highly developed prayer which probably formed a regular part of the temple liturgy – perhaps used as part of an annual festival along with Psalm 24 and other temple material. The prayer acknowledges the tension between affirming the reality of God's presence in the temple and recognizing that 'even heaven and the highest heaven cannot contain God' (6:18). The prayer seeks to reconcile the apparent contradiction by asking God to make his *name* dwell in the temple so that it might be the place in which he is called upon in prayer and praise.

We saw a similar device at work in the story of Moses on Sinai. The *name* of God was revealed to his ears but the *glory* of God was withheld from his sight. This may reflect two ways of envisaging God's presence with his people which were combined when the biblical narratives reached their final form. The one, concerning the *name*, perhaps circulated in the northern kingdom of Israel with its nomadic traditions and the other, concerning the *glory*, was more familiar in the southern kingdom of Judah with its temple in Jerusalem.[8] Nevertheless, we should not overplay their difference. They both have a common root in the closeness *and* the distance of God. The name is revealed and God's nature is known by his name, yet the name simply affirms the transcendence of God over every other name. The glory is manifested and God's presence is experienced in his glory, yet the glory is always a veiled form of his presence and always calls people to fall in worship before the one who is beyond all things.

The temple and its relationship with the glory of God is given a great deal of attention in the prophetic ministry of Ezekiel. Ezekiel was one of the prophets of the Babylonian exile. His prophecies begin with a vision of the temple in which he encounters 'the appearance of the likeness of the glory of the Lord' (1:28). The glory of God then brings Ezekiel a number of visions including the sight of the 'abominations' committed in the temple which cause the glory to depart from the temple. The visions continue and hope returns as he hears the promise of God to revive his people and 'set his sanctuary among them for ever more' (37:27) but not before they have been given a new spirit and a new heart (36:26–8). The prophecies end with a final vision (43–7) in which he sees God's glory return to the temple and from there flows out into every corner of the land bringing healing and justice. The last prophecy tells us that Jerusalem, which will be at the centre of this new creation, will be known by a new name: 'The Lord is there' (48:35).

Ezekiel's vision of the eschatological revelation of the glory of God is paralleled in the exilic and post-exilic prophecies of the book of Isaiah. God will restore his people – he made them 'for his glory' (43:1). In their salvation God's glory will be revealed to all people and extended to all people (66:18–23). The new creation will be one of justice and peace, healing and wholeness (Isa. 65:17–25; see also 35:1–10) in which 'all flesh shall come to worship before me, says the Lord' (66:23). According to this prophetic tradition, when God's purposes in creation are brought to fulfilment, his glory will be fully displayed in three ways. It will be demonstrated in the *revelation* of the true identity of Israel's God as the one creator and redeemer. It will be manifested by the real presence of God *indwelling* his renewed creation causing it to reflect his beauty and splendour. It will be acknowledged in the renewed creation's *celebration of praise* as God is given unending glory.

II GLORY IN CHRIST

The song by Joan Osborne quoted earlier goes on to ask:

> What if God was one of us
> . . . just a stranger on a bus
> trying to make his way home
> . . . back up to heaven all alone
> nobody call him on the phone
> 'Cept for the Pope maybe in Rome?

Deep within the category-shattering experience of early Christian life was the conviction that although Jesus was most definitely 'one of us', he also belonged in some extraordinary way to the reality of God. The theme of the glory of God played a critical part in articulating this belief. As the analysis of *doxa* (the Greek word for glory) in Kittel's *Theological Dictionary of the New Testament* states, 'New Testament usage itself takes a decisive step by using in relation to Christ a word which was used in relation to God'.[9] Many of these references had their origin in some form of encounter with the risen Christ and led to statements of worship to him.

Stephen's defence before the Jewish authorities in Acts 7 begins by talking about 'the God of glory' who appeared to Abraham. It ends with a vision in which Stephen effectively sets his own death sentence. He saw 'the glory of God and Jesus standing at the right hand of God' and then prayed to his exalted Lord. The phrase 'standing at the right hand of God' was an allusion to Psalm 110. Much use was made of this psalm by the New Testament and post-Apostolic writers. Its use was traced back to Jesus himself (Mark 12:35–7) and it became increasingly used in hymns and confessions of faith to celebrate the Lordship of Christ. David Hay concluded his thorough study of this usage with these words: 'Early Christians chiefly employed the psalm to articulate the supreme glory, the divine transcendence, of Jesus, through whom salvation was mediated. It was primarily used as a symbol not of his saving work but of his ultimate significance.'[10]

It is quite possible that Paul's description of Christ as 'the Lord of glory' (1 Cor. 2:8) and his claim that we have been given 'the light of the knowledge of the glory of God in the face of Jesus Christ' (2 Cor. 4:6) derived from his Damascus road experience when he heard Christ speaking to him out of a heavenly light that was so dazzling it blinded him. The persecutor who had consented to Stephen's death on the grounds of his blasphemous association of Jesus with God's glory was himself thrown to the ground by the overwhelming manifestation of Christ's presence surrounded by divine glory. Later, using all the skills of his theological mind, he claimed that the face of God, which had been partially, though correctly, discerned by Jacob, Moses and all the prophets, as one of steadfast love and faithfulness, had come to full light in the face of Christ (2 Cor. 4:6).

The Pauline epistles, Acts, Hebrews and the Synoptic Gospels generally relate the glory of Christ to *his heavenly state*. It is as Christ moves from the cross, through the resurrection and to the exaltation that his true identity as the Lord who shares the divine glory is made clear. The Johannine writings, however, relate Jesus' glory to the *whole of his life* – and do so by using the idea of God's face in the sophisticated form of the vision of God. In the prologue to the Gospel, John affirms the Jewish belief in God's invisibility: 'No one has ever seen God' (1:18; see also 5:37 and 1 John 4:12). Yet he also claims the Christian conviction that 'the only Son, who is close to the Father's heart, has made him known' (1:18). In Christ, God's Word – his grace (steadfast love) and truth (faithfulness) – has been embodied, made flesh, so that we can 'see his glory' (1:14). Christ's miracles are signs revealing the glory he shares with God as love (ch. 5), light (ch. 9) and life (ch. 11). To come to Christ is to come to the Father (14:6). To honour Christ is to honour the Father (5:23). To see Christ is to see the Father (14:9). Nevertheless, the vision of God's glory in Christ remains veiled until the final events of Jesus' earthly life and is not completely revealed until his coming again (1 John 3:2). Before he dies Jesus prays that his disciples may see the glory he had with the Father before the world was made (17:5). Michael Ramsey's masterful study of the glory of God continues the story:

> The prayer is ended. The Passion begins. Throughout the narrative John shows that the prayer is being answered and the Son is being glorified. In the garden the soldiers who come to arrest Jesus fall to the ground awestruck at His majesty. In the judgment hall it is Jesus who is the judge and Pilate is his craven prisoner. Before the people Jesus is shewn forth as King, in the purple and the crown of thorns; and King indeed He is. Master of His destiny Jesus carries His own Cross to Calvary, for He has power to lay down His life and power to take it again. On Calvary He reigns, ordering the future for the mother and the disciple, crying 'it is accomplished', fulfilling the Scriptures, and freely surrendering His spirit to the Father. So the hour came that the Son of Man should be glorified, and the corn of wheat fell to the earth and died.[11]

After death comes burial – but burial with a difference as far as John is concerned. B.F. Westcott notes in his commentary that John's description of Christ's tomb is evocative of the temple, as if to say that the dwelling place of God is the only fitting dwelling place for the one whose death revealed such divine glory.[12]

Jesus' glorious dying and glorious resting are followed by his glorious rising as Mary's despair, Thomas' doubt and Peter's betrayal are transformed into joy, belief and unswerving commitment. John folds the giving of the Spirit into the one glorious event of Jesus' death and resurrection. The disciples receive the Holy Spirit and are commissioned for Christ's work (20:22–3), consecrated by the same self-giving which marked the life of Christ and revealed his true glory as Son of the Father (17:17–19).

The connection between Christ's glory and his cross, so carefully developed by John, runs throughout the New Testament. It can be seen clearly in the account of the transfiguration in Mark, Luke and Matthew. For a moment the veil is lifted from Christ's identity. He is transfigured. The Greek verb (*metamorphoun*) means a profound change of form. Matthew locates the change in Jesus' face which 'shone like the sun' (17:2). As Jesus and the three disciples return from the mountain in Mark and Matthew, Jesus tells them not to tell anyone what has happened until the resurrection. They had anticipated the end. He then goes on to prophesy about his death. Luke tells us that in their conversation with Jesus, Moses and Elijah had told him of the coming events in Jerusalem (9:31). Their dialogue was the subject of a moving contemplation by the seventeenth-century Anglican bishop, Joseph Hall, before the Royal Court of James I:

> A strange opportunity . . . when his head shone with glory, to tell him how it must bleed with thorns; when his face shone like the sun, to tell him it must be blubbered and spat upon; when his garments glistened with celestial brightness, to tell him they must be stripped and divided . . . and whilst he was Transfigured on the Mount, to tell him how he must be Disfigured on the Cross![13]

The staggering claim of the New Testament is that, as Kittel's dictionary puts it, 'the *doxa* [glory] derives from his death'.[14] If we are to take this with the seriousness the New Testament demands, if we are to say that Jesus' glory really is revealed through the cross and that this glory – his true identity – is that he shares the glory of God, we must go on to say that God's own glory – God's true nature as God – is proclaimed *on and through the cross.*

John Donne, a contemporary of Joseph Hall, wrote a poem about Christ's death called 'Good Friday, 1613, Riding Westward'. It pictures someone who is riding from the East and therefore missing the sight of the rising of the sun:

> There I should see a Sunne, by rising set,
> And by that setting endlesse day beget;
> But that Christ on this Crosse, did rise and fall,
> Sinne had eternally benighted all.
> Yet dare I' almost be glad, I do not see
> That spectacle of too much weight for mee.
> Who sees Gods face, that is selfe life, must dye;
> What a death were it then to see God dye?[15]

A hundred years later another poet, Charles Wesley, in a poem based on the story of Jacob wrestling in the night, found that there is life and not death in seeing the dying of God.

> Yield to me Now – for I am weak;
> But confident in Self-despair:
> Speak to my Heart, in Blessings speak,
> Be conquer'd by my Instant Prayer,
> Speak, or Thou never hence shalt move,
> And tell me, if Thy Name is *Love.*
>
> 'Tis Love, 'tis Love! Thou diedst for Me,
> I hear Thy Whisper in my Heart.
> The Morning breaks, the Shadows flee:
> Pure *universal Love* Thou art,

To me, to All Thy Bowels move,
Thy Nature, and Thy Name is *Love*.

My Prayer hath Power with *God*; the Grace
Unspeakable I now receive,
Thro' Faith I see Thee Face to Face,
I see Thee Face to Face, and live:
In vain I have not wept, and strove,
Thy Nature, and Thy Name is *Love*.[16]

In the recent decades of this century two theologians of very different styles have given repeated and radical expression to the significance of the cross for all our talk about God. The theology of Jürgen Moltmann, the German Reformed theologian, revolves around the full horror of human suffering and refuses to define God in any other way than in the agony of Christ's experience of desolation on the cross:

> When the crucified Jesus is called the 'image of the invisible God', the meaning is that *this* is God, and God is like *this*. God is not greater than he is in this humiliation. God is not more glorious than he is in this self-surrender. God is not more powerful than he is in this helplessness. God is not more divine than he is in this humanity.[17]

The theology of Hans Urs von Balthasar, the Swiss Roman Catholic theologian, revolves around the beauty of God's being but finds this most fully displayed in the event of the cross:

> It is precisely now that the Word who has been reduced to silence receives his absolute transparency to the Father, who expresses himself in him in a way without precedent. The whole Johannine understanding of the Logos is marked by this starting-point, and rightly: for the one who bears such extreme suffering . . . must be a uniquely suitable medium

for this power of the Father as he gives himself expression, a medium that shows itself, in its capacity to bear the burden, to be itself divine. Only God himself can go right to the end of the abandonment by God. Only he has the freedom to do this.[18]

This is why the Church declares that Christ is 'of one being (*homoousios*) with the Father'. Father and Son are not, as Arius argued, 'altogether dissimilar (*anomoioi*) from each other in their levels of glory'.[19] Rather, the self-giving love of Christ *is* the divine glory of the one God. The true identity of God was revealed on the cross because the real presence of God was upon the cross.

This conviction belongs to the essence of New Testament and was seen by its writers as consistent in principle with the way God had revealed himself to be. The God of Israel, whose heart burnt with compassion for his suffering people (Exod. 3:7–9), was present in the humiliation of their history as well as in the splendour of his heaven (Isa. 57:15). The point of departure for the New Testament writers was their claim that the principles by which God had defined himself had been worked out in radical practice in the person of Jesus. The God whose transcendent rule over all things is shown in his freedom to serve his people in love became the suffering servant emptying himself, giving up all, pouring himself out in human death, for the one who bears human form and exercises human will still bears the divine name and exercises divine Lordship (Phil. 2:6–11). The God who alone is the first and the last (Isa. 44:6) is one with the Christ who has been through death (Rev. 1:17–18) for amidst the throne of the one God there stands the Lamb who has been slain (Rev. 5:6). The glory of the Lord which was to be revealed to all people (Isa. 40:5) *is* the lifting up of the Son of Man upon the cross for the salvation of the world (Isa. 52:13, John 3:14–15, 12:32), for this is the time when

141

the Son makes the Father known and in so doing makes himself known as the only Son of the Father who is one with him. This is the eschatological demonstration of *who God is* about which the prophets prophesied and the people prayed. St Francis' questions 'Who are you God?' and 'Who am I?' are fully and finally answered. God is the one who goes to the cross to save his people and I am one of the people for whom God goes to the cross.

III GLORY THROUGH THE SPIRIT

Just as the application of the word glory to Christ played a critical part in the definition of his divinity, so the theme of glory was instrumental to the recognition of the Spirit's divinity. An influential text was John 16:13–15 which talks of the Spirit of truth coming to bring knowledge and experience of the glory of the Son and the Father. Athanasius, the Cappadocians and other orthodox theologians argued that only if the Spirit participates in the same glory as the Son and the Father, can he reveal and relate us to the glory of the Son and the Father. This is why Basil was so insistent that the Nicene Creed of 325 should be expanded to include an acknowledgement of the divine glory of the Spirit and why he so resolutely defended his use of the doxology which clearly ascribed glory to the Spirit together with the Father and the Son.

We saw earlier how *glory* and *face* are essentially eschatological concepts. The Midrash, a collection of rabbinic interpretations of Scripture, shows that Jewish faith was clear about the content of God's promises and expectant about its fulfilment: 'in the coming aeon . . . I will disclose myself in my glory to all Israel, and they shall see and live for ever'.[20] As we have also seen, in the New Testament *glory* and *face* became intrinsically related to Jesus and the events surrounding him. The theological and experiential link between Jesus and the eschatological manifestation of the glory of God was the resurrection and the pouring out of the Spirit. In these momentous events eschatological time had begun. For the Spirit was the eschatological power and presence of God to be poured out in the last days when God's purposes, including his promise to raise his people from the dead, would be fulfilled.

The Greek Orthodox theologian, John Zizioulas, describes the Spirit's eschatological identity and the Spirit's eschatological work in this way: 'the Spirit is the *beyond* history, and when he acts in history, he does so to bring history into the last days, the *eschaton* . . . The Spirit makes of Christ the eschatological being, the "last Adam" '.[21] Jesus is literally the Christ (*Christos*), which means the anointed one. He is anointed with the Spirit at his baptism. He heals, exorcises, teaches, prays, praises and lives the obedient life, even to death, through the Spirit. He is raised from death by the power of the Spirit who is as active in the new creation as he was in the old. The humanity which Jesus shares with us is fashioned by the Spirit into the perfection which allows him to ascend into the holiness of God's presence to see God's glory and to be 'crowned with glory and honour' (Heb. 2:9). Such a sight of and share in the glory of God can only happen to the person of Jesus on the other side of the resurrection, because the transformation of human nature required for the experience of God's glory involves human physicality as well as human spirituality. Eschatological salvation is the renewal of the whole being of a human person.

As well as being anointed with the Spirit. Jesus baptizes with the Spirit. He does not direct us to our *own* baptism, he takes us into *his* baptism, *his* anointing and so draws us into *his* eschatological life – his new humanity which ever lives before his Father in the Spirit. Because our participation in Christ is truly a participation in the *eschaton*, in that it is a share in the new life of Christ given by the Spirit, it is a participation in the glory of God. In a very real sense, of course, this participation in God's glory still belongs to the future. 'Christ in us' is 'the hope of glory' (Col. 1:27). When his glory is fully and unambiguously revealed, ours will be also (Col. 3:4; Rom. 8:17). On that day we will share in his resurrection and our bodies 'of humiliation' will be transformed so that they 'may be conformed to the body of his glory' (Phil. 3:21). By the Spirit God will raise us into the full reality of the new creation begun in Christ. In another way, though, our participation in the glory of God is a present possession, for even now 'the Spirit of glory, which is the Spirit of God, is resting on [us]' (1 Pet. 4:14). The Spirit in the believer is the first fruit (*aparchē*) of the coming harvest, the down payment (*arrabōn*) of the promised inheritance guaranteeing the fullness of the future by bringing it partly into the present.

The relationship between the present and the future is brought out clearly by Paul in 2 Corinthians 3 and 4. Here and now we are bearers of God's glory in increasing degrees (3:18), and yet we are waiting for 'an eternal weight of glory beyond all measure' (4:17) which will be ours when we are raised into Christ's presence (4:14). Paul goes on to relate the theme of glory to the theme of face, holding the work of the Spirit and the work of Christ together in the closest connection. Generally Paul distinguishes clearly between the Spirit and Christ. But here, on two occasions, he seems to equate them: 'the Lord is the Spirit' (3:17–18). It seems that he does so in order to emphasize that Christ belongs to the realm of the Spirit. In Christ the purposes of God have been so fully fulfilled that the Spirit's eschatological work of creating the new humanity is complete in him. We participate in this new humanity in as much as we relate by faith to Christ. Paul uses the language of face and sight to describe this relationship by faith. Christ is the perfected image of God (3:18, 4:4). From the beauty of his face shines the glory of God (3:18, 4:6). As we respond to the 'ministry of the Spirit' (3:18) and 'turn to the Lord' (3:16) the veil which masks his true identity for us is lifted and we see him as he is, as Lord, sharing the glory of God. Through the ongoing faith relationship we are transformed into a closer approximation to Christ, the image of God. Paul says that we are being changed from 'one degree of glory to another'. Later, Irenaeus said that 'the glory of God is a person fully alive, and the life of humanity is to see God'.[22] God is glorified in the perfection of his creation and to be perfected into that which God wills us to be is to be glorified, for then we arrive at our true identity as a people prepared to participate fully in the love and joy of the life of God.

The eschatological fulfilment of this process is described in 1 John in terms of the final coming of Christ when he will be so fully revealed that 'we will be like him, for we will see him as he is' (3:2). The true meaning of our status as God's children will then become clear as we participate fully in the life of Christ. Christ's prayer that we may share in his glory will be fulfilled, for in Christ we will share in the intimacy of his relationship of love with the Father and we will be bound together in a relationship of love with each other (John 17:22-3). All of this happens of course by the work of the Spirit who is *now* transforming us into Christ's likeness and who will *then* complete his work in the coming of Christ which will be nothing less than the arrival of the new creation inhabited by God himself (Rev. 21:3) and shining with his splendour.

The Spirit's work of transforming God's people is intrinsically related to the experience of worship. The Spirit is the one who enables us to worship because the Spirit brings us into fellowship with Christ and therefore with each other and with his Father. As we worship we enter into the movement of Christ's self-giving to the Father through the Spirit

(Heb. 9:14), which was the cause of his glorification in his death, and into the movement of his receiving of life and power through the Spirit, which was the cause of his glorification in his birth and baptism. Both movements are grounded in the eternal movement of the Son who is eternally begotten by the Father by the breath of the Spirit. They are extended to us in the dynamic of worship as we hold out our hands and hearts in worship to offer all that we long to give to God and to receive all that God longs to give to us. By glorifying God, we are glorified because we are becoming what we have been created to be.

As Moltmann has written, '*the Father* creates the world out of his eternal love through *the Son,* for the purpose of finding a response to his love in time, in the power of *the Holy Spirit,* which binds together what is in itself different'.[23] We are that response in time. We therefore participate in what Moltmann calls the 'doxological trinity', by which he means the life of the Trinity as it becomes in the fulfilment of God's creative purposes. In order for the exercise of love to succeed, it must evoke a free response in which love is received and returned. Hence, the love of God expressed in the creative process is brought to completion and perfection in our praise: and God is glorified.

The last chapter of the book of Revelation ends with a vision of the eschatological city of God. This city has no need of a temple for God has made his home in its streets – he is its temple. His faithful servants gather around 'the throne of God and of the Lamb' and, finally and fully, they 'see his face' (22:3–4; see also 1 Cor. 13:12). The Church of this present age, with the excited expectation and yearning impatience of a bride longing for her marriage, joins with the voice of the Spirit crying out for the consummation of God's future, saying, 'Amen. Come, Lord Jesus!' (22:20)

6

oooooooooo

The Invitation of Christ

'Come to me . . .'
(Matthew 11:28)

I A PERSONAL INTRODUCTION

'Have you invited Christ into your life?' This is a very familiar question for anyone formed in the evangelical tradition of the Church. I can remember being asked it at the tender age of twelve. Even then I knew what the question meant and I knew what was the honest answer. It was 'No, I haven't'. I had not personally and consciously welcomed Christ into my life in the sense of a decision to give my life to Christ and allow him to live his life in me. Attracted by the lives of those I knew who had made that sort of response, I found myself able to do it also. My life changed. It has never been the same since. Many years later I met a distinguished Anglo-Catholic Oxford College chaplain who was clearly somewhat tired of the zeal and, I imagine, insensitivity of some of his evangelical students. He said, 'They are always asking if I have invited Jesus into my life. I've now begun to reply, "I'm not sure about that but I do know that I have been invited into the life of Christ, and that is where I am." '

In a very interesting lecture delivered over twenty years ago now, Herbert Ryan, an American Roman Catholic, analysed the English spiritual tradition and came to the conclusion that the primary question with which it has been

147

preoccupied is, 'Where is Christ today and how may I be in union with him?'[1] He surveyed a range of English spiritual writers from the eighth to the fourteenth centuries and claimed that 'the unifying element of Anglican [by which he meant English] spirituality is the integration of the individual believer into the life of Christ'.[2] For example, in her thirteenth revelation Julian of Norwich describes how Jesus reveals himself to those who seek him saying, 'My beloved, I am glad that you have come to me. In all your trouble I have been with you. Now you can see how I love you. We are made one in blessedness'.[3] Similarly the prayers of Anselm of Canterbury are deeply devotional towards Christ. Anselm felt himself to be so deeply bound to the person of Christ and so deeply dependent upon the work of Christ that he called himself the son of Jesus and referred to Christ as his Father and even as his Mother. Also Richard Rolle's *The Fire of Love* is strongly Christocentric. Rolle talks of how the 'elect soul is completely absorbed in his longing to love Christ' and how 'Christ alone transforms himself into his beloved'.[4]

Ryan went on to argue that the Prayer Book of the Church of England was so successful as an experiment in common prayer because it remained true to this tradition. It sought to nurture the believer in a deeper participation in the life of Christ through prayer and to encourage the Christian citizen in a consistent expression of the life of Christ in public and private duty. Although not everyone, including many Anglicans, would be quite as enthusiastic about the achievements of the Prayer Book, Ryan is right in noting the way the *Book of Common Prayer* properly focused on the person of Christ and our life in him. This can be seen very clearly in the Prayer of Humble Access. One of the great prayers of the English Prayer Book tradition, compiled by Thomas Cranmer, it was included in the first of his reforms of the Mass in 1548. Apart from a few changes it has survived various liturgical revisions and remains a prayer much loved by Anglicans and many others. Its contemporary form concludes by asking 'that we may evermore dwell in him [Christ] and he in us'.[5] Cranmer did not just create the prayer out of nothing. He compiled a pastiche of phrases from a number of biblical and liturgical sources and so managed to craft an elegant vehicle for that particular strain of spirituality voiced much earlier by Anselm when he prayed (again before receiving communion):

> May I be incorporated into your body . . .
> So that I may be your member and you may be my head,
> and that I may remain in you and you in me.[6]

Here are both invitations. We are invited to step into the life of Christ, to live our life in him, and we are invited to allow Christ to enter our lives, to live his life in us. We are in Christ and Christ is in us.

Richard Hooker, whose life began just before Cranmer's violently ended, continued to focus on the biblical and experiential heart of the Eucharist. He tried to cut through the sixteenth century's sharply differing views of the way in which Christ is present in the sacrament by pointing to 'a general agreement concerning that which alone is material, namely the *real participation* of Christ and life in his body and blood *by means of this sacrament*'.[7] The tradition continued into the post-Reformation English spirituality. It was taught in the devotional manuals, encapsulated in the use of 'Holy Communion' as the preferred name for the sacrament and celebrated in the writings of various poets. 'By way of nourishment and strength, Thou creep'st into my breast', wrote George Herbert in the seventeenth century,[8] 'But chiefly here my soul is fed, with fulness of immortal bread', sang Charles Wesley in the eighteenth century.[9] 'Now Thou dost bid me come and sup with Thee, Now

Thou dost make me lean upon thy breast', prayed Christina Rossetti in the nineteenth.[10]

Although the English, and particularly the Anglican, tradition can claim a particular merit in seeking to concentrate theological and devotional attention on the reality of our communion with Christ in the Eucharist, belief in the eucharistic participation in the life of Christ, of course, is shared, as Hooker sought to show, by the whole Church. As a university chaplain working in an ecumenical team I was often asked by Roman Catholic students to talk to various groups about the Anglican understanding of Christ's presence in the Eucharist. I used to take Thérèse of Lisieux's *Autobiography* with me and read the account of her first communion. Thérèse was a young nineteenth-century nun whose writings have had a significant influence on Roman Catholic spirituality in this century.

> What comfort it brought to me, that first kiss our Lord imprinted on my soul! A lover's kiss; I knew that I was loved, and I, in my turn, told him that I loved him, and was giving myself to him for all eternity. There were no demands on me; there had been no struggles, no sacrifices. It was a long time since we had exchanged looks, he and I, insignificant though I was, and we had understood one another. And now it wasn't a question of looks; something had melted away, and there were no longer two of us – Thérèse had simply disappeared, like a drop lost in the ocean; Jesus only was left, my Master, my King.
>
> So deep was my joy, so overpowering, that I couldn't contain myself; before long, tears of happiness were pouring down my cheeks to the astonishment of my companions. . . . They didn't realise what happens when all the joys of heaven come flooding into a human heart; how difficult it is for that heart, still in exile, to stand the strain of the impact without finding relief in tears.[11]

Here and elsewhere Thérèse does not try to define the way in which Christ is present, neither does she seem very interested in Christ's presence apart from the reception of the elements. She simply enjoys the reality of the joyful exchange in which Christ gives himself to her and she gives herself to Christ. Thérèse helped me to show that at the heart of Anglican and Roman Catholic theology of the Eucharist there lies a common conviction that Christ invites us to receive his gift of himself to us. Indeed, the whole of Christian life and worship is a continual process of encountering Christ and responding to his call to share his life more fully. In the next section we shall examine the theological basis of our participation in Christ and then explore some of the implications which follow for our understanding of worship. In the final section we shall return to the Eucharist to ground some of this thinking in the realities of the liturgical life Sunday by Sunday.

II A THEOLOGICAL ANALYSIS

The theological basis of our participation in Christ

In the last chapter we talked about God creating the world in order to find *a response to his love in time.* Humanity, especially in its prayer of trust and song of praise, is to voice that response. However, we know the biblical story faces the fact that we are flawed, unable by ourselves to enter into the perfection of his presence and incapable in ourselves of worshipping with the pureness of life required by the purity of God. This is the liturgical dilemma which runs through the pages of the Old Testament. Created to glorify God we have been corrupted by sin. Called to walk and talk with God we find we have to hide from him – his holiness is too much for us to bear.

The horns of the dilemma are dramatically exposed in

the account of the inauguration of Aaron and his sons as priests in Leviticus 9 and 10. After the new priests offer the first sacrifices according to the strict instructions of Moses, God's glory then appears to the people and literally consumes the sacrifice, confirming that their worship is acceptable. There is a genuine encounter with the presence of God but it happens within a prescribed context in which sin is acknowledged and atonement sought – although even then the manifestation of God's presence is only temporary and, it would seem, terrifying. Later, Aaron's sons presume to offer a sacrifice of their choosing in their own way and not according to the command of God. The presence of God again appears but this time it overwhelms them and they fall to the ground in death rather than worship. Moses has to explain what has happened. All he can do is to appeal to the holiness of God. God is so unlike us, so perfect, that he can only be approached on his own terms. By ourselves and of ourselves we are like straw before a fire. We cannot bear the power of his presence.

The dilemma is intensified in the prophetic tradition from the eighth century onwards with its critique of the priestly system. YHWH, the prophets claim, demands not just *ritual* purity but *moral* purity. It is not simply a case of performing the liturgical actions properly, they must be accompanied with the proper moral attitudes in both the offering of the sacrifices and the ordering of society. Anything less remains under God's judgement. It does not meet the demands of his holiness. It is not holy (separated from sin) because the people offering it are not holy (separated from sin) in the inner fabric of their lives and the outer structure of their society. Just when the prophets seem to be asking the impossible of the priests and people, we hear them prophesying that God will provide the answer. The prophetic hope, as we have seen, is that a time is coming when all people will be able to offer a 'pure offering' (Mal.

1:11) in the presence of the perfect God because they will have been transformed by God. They will have a new spirit and a new heart (Ezek. 36:26–8). They will know the Lord and will freely and willingly live according to his way (Jer. 31:33–4). They will dwell in a righteous land (Isa. 65:17–25).

We have also seen that for the New Testament writers this prophetic hope has come to fulfilment in Christ. He is the one in whom the new life, new knowledge and new kingdom are to be found. He lives obediently, prays intimately and he brings healing and peace. He dies obediently, in prayer, for the sake of the kingdom. 'Truly', says the centurion, 'this man was God's son' (Mark 15:39). This person is as a human being is meant to be – holy, as God is holy. And what is more his holiness is not something just *for him.* It becomes, by his death, resurrection and ascension, something *for us* and, through the coming of the Spirit, something *in us.* Through him and in him we too can be holy and stand in the presence of God.

As we saw in chapter 4, the Church came to perceive the full depths of these events and to claim that (as Thomas Torrance summarizes it) 'in Jesus we have none other than the being of God himself in space and time'.[12] The faith of the Church is that God assumes humanity in order to reconcile it to himself. The distance between the eternal Son and the Father in the life of God, which is implicit in the notion of their distinct hypostases or identities, is extended by the Spirit to include our humanity in order to liberate it from the death of disobedience to the freedom of his life of love. Hence, in Jesus the dynamic of the eternal life of the Son inhabits humanity. The Son is eternally given being by the Father through the breath of the Spirit, and by his eternal reception of being from the Father through the Spirit, the Son is in an eternal movement of devotion towards the Father. In Jesus the eternal Son takes on our humanity to live out these eternal movements in the form of human life. He is born of Mary by the will of the Father through the action of the Spirit. He is appointed and anointed for messianic ministry by the voice of the Father and the touch of the Spirit. He teaches and heals, resists and delivers by the word of the Father through the power of the Spirit. He dies in obedience to the Father through the movement of the Spirit. He is raised by the command of the Father through the power of the Spirit.

This catalogue of stages in the life of Christ should be enough to show that Jesus' humanity was not instantly perfected simply by virtue of the incarnation. It was an ongoing process which began at his conception and birth, continued through his life and death and was completed in his resurrection and ascension. The humanity which God assumed at the conception of Christ had to be reformed and refashioned by the obedience of the eternal Son to the Father through the Spirit now being lived out in the full reality and conditions of human life. The temptation and Gethsemane narratives make it clear that Jesus was fully engaged with the human realities of temptation and fear. The difference between him and us was that although tempted in *every way* as we are, he remained so consistently open to the transforming work of the Spirit (who drove him into the desert and directed him towards the cross) that he remained faithful to his Father and did not sin (Heb. 4:15).

At his baptism Jesus had been proclaimed the Son of God and anointed by the Spirit for the messianic work of the kingdom of God. His ministry was one of radical obedience in which he did the Father's work and spoke the Father's word through the enabling of the Spirit. His death was a continuation of his messianic mission. As the righteous and anointed servant of God he gave himself to suffer for the sins of his people. He went to his death to represent God's people under God's judgement. He went to the cross where the accused and accursed hang in alienation from God. He went to the place of death, the place where humanity had found itself as it had turned from the life of God. He bore the awful reality of being excluded from the presence of the holy God.

In order to probe more deeply into this mystery I want to turn to the book of Hebrews for help.[13] Hebrews applies Psalm 40:6–8 to Jesus:

> Therefore, when Christ came into the world, he said:
> 'Sacrifice and offering you did not desire,
> but a body you prepared for me,
> with burnt offerings and sin offerings
> you were not pleased.
> Then I said, "Here I am – it is written about me in the
>   scroll –
> I have come to do your will, O God." '
> First he said, 'Sacrifices and offerings, burnt offerings and sin offerings you did not desire, nor were you pleased with them' (although the law required them to be made). Then he said, 'Here I am, I have come to do your will.' He sets aside the first to establish the second. And by that will, we have been made holy through the sacrifice of the body of Jesus Christ once for all. (10:5–10 NIV)

The writer's point is that 'Christ came into the world' to do God's will. With the benefit of later trinitarian theology we can fill this out by saying that the eternal Son became incarnate in order to reproduce the pattern of his obedient self-giving to the Father through the Spirit *as a human being*. But there is more to say. For the obedience which took Jesus to his death was a *priestly obedience*. He died not just as our brother, sharing our humanity but as our priest, called and commissioned to act for us. The will which he obeys is that we should be 'made holy through the sacrifice of the body of Jesus Christ once for all'. He went to the cross as our priest to offer the sacrifice of himself, suffering the pain of our forsakenness by God and bearing the judgement of God upon us. The cross therefore has a double dimension. Jesus' obedient self-giving not only establishes the perfection of *his* humanity (5:8–9, 7:28), it also creates the conditions for *us* to share in his perfection by receiving his priestly ministry (5:8–9).

We can expand on the double aspect of the cross by considering its liturgical or doxological character. Jesus' dying in obedience to the Father through the Spirit is an act of worship in which he pours himself out in devoted duty. He surrenders all to God in one act of complete self-giving of body, mind and spirit. But his death is not a suicide. It is not primarily an attempt on Jesus' part to glorify God by showing that there is nothing he will hold back from God – not even his own life. Rather, Jesus seeks to glorify God in his death by offering in his own person a priestly oblation through which we can be made holy. To be holy we need to be forgiven. To be forgiven we need to confess our sin truly and fully. Jesus confesses our sin truly and fully on the cross. He does so not simply in thought and word but *in deed.* He goes to the cross to acknowledge our sin before God and to accept the rightness of God in judging sin. To be made holy we need to be re-formed. To be re-formed we need to be reconstituted and renewed. Jesus does this on the cross by taking the old form of humanity to its death so that the new form of humanity will be perfected in him and made available to all. The irony here is worth noting. In his dying as in his living, it is precisely as Jesus overcomes the sinfulness of the old humanity, as he stands in judgement over it, taking God's side against it, that he renews and reconstitutes it, re-forming it into the image of God. Jesus' death is then both an act of *personal offering* and worship to God which seals the perfection of his humanity and at the same time the act of *priestly ministry* through which we too can be perfected.

156

Although the critical point in Jesus' ministry comes at the cross, the climactic point, as far as Hebrews is concerned, happens at the ascension. For Hebrews the ascension is the great liturgical moment for humanity. It is the pinnacle of Christ's redemptive work because a human being enters the heavenly place of God's presence and sits at his right hand. Jesus remains our brother. His humanity is not discarded. But it has been glorified. Jesus remains our priest also. He enters 'heaven itself, now to appear in the presence of God on our behalf' (9:24). When Aaron ministered in the earthly sanctuary he wore the names of the tribes of Israel on his breast piece – the liturgical vestment covering his heart. As Christ ascends to minister in the heavenly sanctuary he carries our names on his heart before the presence of God just as surely as he bore them in his priestly sacrifice on the cross. Furthermore, he comes before the holiest presence of God as 'the pioneer and perfecter of our faith' (12:2), or as Luther put it in his commentary on Hebrews, 'the ferryman' ready to take us with him.[14] The invitation of the book of Hebrews is to go where he goes.

How, though, can we go with him? Hebrews suggests that we do so by participating or sharing in his righteous and risen life in three interrelated phases. The first phase is initiatory. Through baptism and by faith we are included in and receive for ourselves the priestly ministry of Christ. Acknowledging that he died our death so that we might live his life, his holiness is *applied to us* and we are welcomed into the holiness of God. Our sins are forgiven and we are set free to worship (10:19–23).

The second is consecratory. Through the ongoing process of Christian living and Christian worshipping Christ's holiness becomes *formed in us*. Our holiness always remains relative to Christ's – in that it is his holiness which he grafts into us and crafts within us – but it is an increasingly real holiness. It is a personal, even if still highly provisional,

157

perfection. We should expect nothing less. If, through our participation in Christ, we have come, as Hebrews says we have (12:18–24), into the very presence of God, then such an encounter cannot leave us unchanged.

The third is eschatological. At the consummation of God's kingdom we will be *transformed into Christ's likeness.* We will be like him – holy and righteous. In fact this eschatological state is the basis of our justification (the counting of us as holy) and the basis of our sanctification (the making of us holy), for God sees us now as we will be then and brings something of that future glory into the present reality of our lives. The appearance of Christ 'a second time' (9:20) refers to the full and final manifestation of his saving work. At this point in the future of our world's history God's creative purposes will have been fulfilled. The Sabbath will have come and we will be with God, enjoying his presence in his perfected creation for ever (4:9–11).

Implications for our understanding of worship

So far we have said that humanity has come to its perfected form in Christ. We have also said that in his life, death and continuing ministry in heaven, Christ is our high priest. We have said further that by the grace of God we are invited to participate in the holy life of the ascended Christ. It is now time to draw out some of the implications of this for our understanding of worship. First, we need to say that the perfect human prayer and the perfect human praise are to be found on the lips of Jesus *our brother.* He is the perfect worshipper in the presence of the perfect God.

Secondly, we need to say that because Christ is *God's Son,* 'the reflection of God's glory and the exact imprint of God's very being' (1:3), the words of his human worship are of the same fundamental grammar and the same fundamental semantic content as the words of the divine life of worship.

The incarnation links divine language to human language. Jesus is the Word made flesh. He lives out divine life and speaks out divine speech in human life and human language.[15]

Third, we need to say that because he is *our priest*, and because we are invited to receive his priestly ministry for us and to be included in his holy humanity, our worship is a participation in his worship. Christ is the 'minister [*leitourgos*] of the new sanctuary', the *leader* of our worship. He proclaims God and praises God 'in the midst of the congregation' (2:12). 'Christ leads our songs, and is the chief composer of our hymns' as Calvin puts it in his commentary on Hebrews.[16] He calls us to join his voice and to share in his song. God in Christ gives us words for worship. They are divine words which have been accurately translated into human language by the movement to us in the incarnation and they are words which are authentically returned to the divine life by the movement to God in the priesthood of Christ.

We are not saying anything new here. We are just underlining the comment of the Scottish ordinand recounted in chapter 2 about worship being 'joining Jesus as he praises his Father'. Nevertheless it is worth pausing to note that this is not the usual understanding of worship found in most of our congregations. I often wonder whether the ordinand had been taught by the Scottish theologian James Torrance who helpfully sets out two contrasting views of worship.[17] The first is the typical one held, we have to admit, by most of us at least some of the time. It assumes that worship is something which *we do*. We sing and pray. We listen to the sermon and we contribute to the collection. According to this view worship is essentially a *task*.[18] At its best it may be a grateful response to all that God has done for us in Christ but because it is *our* response which *we* make it remains a task nonetheless and can, as Torrance says, 'engender weariness'. The other view begins with the great themes of the gospel. It recognizes that our worship is a participation in the priestly prayer and praise of Christ through the enabling of the Spirit. According to this view worship is essentially a *gift*. Alan Torrance, James' son, echoes his father's perspective: 'Worship is not some valiant subjective response, therefore. It is a gift of grace which is realised vicariously in Christ and which is received and participated in by the Spirit'.[19]

An architectural illustration might help to compare the two understandings of worship. Despite the devotion of the worshippers who gather at the Wailing Wall in Jerusalem, there is something very unsatisfactory about it as a place of prayer. It is just a wall. People pray before it and place their petitions in its crevices. The first view of worship can feel like that. We are fairly sure we are in the right place for our prayer. We seem to be doing the right things. We work hard to engage our emotions and we even use our bodies to help us. But still we feel on the outside and can only hope that our prayers are getting through the wall. The second view of worship is more like a cruciform cathedral. We can only enter it as we step onto the shape of the cross and walk the way of the cross. As we do so we find ourselves in a building of enormous proportions, full of beauty and elegance. Better still is the Liebfrauenkirche in Trier with its clearly cruciform pattern set within a circular shape; it is like a Celtic cross. The circle expresses the eternal trinitarian life of God into which we are invited to take our part through the person of the Son. He takes on our humanity and gives himself to death on the cross, so that by his sacrifice we may be made holy (Heb. 10:10). Irenaeus said that 'for his immense love's sake, the Word of God . . . was made that which we are, in order that he might perfect us to be what he is'.[20] The Word, who is *by nature* the child of God eternally generated by the Father, took on our humanity and became our brother, so that we might become children of God *by grace*, adopted by the Father through our union with him.

Worship is a gift we are invited to receive. We are invited to join the prayer and praise of Christ and to allow our voice to be perfected in his. It is within this framework that I understand the words from the Statement produced by the Anglican–Roman Catholic International Commission which became a source of some contention for some: 'In the eucharistic prayer . . . [we] enter into the movement of his self-offering'.[21] Some have felt that this undermines the completion and sufficiency of the cross by implying that in some way it is re-enacted in the sacramental action of the Church. Of course nothing can repeat or compete with Christ's sacrifice. It is because of what he did there and then in the offering of his life at Calvary that we can share here and now in the offering of his praise in heaven. It is because he bore the judgement of God upon the sin of our old humanity and allowed the Spirit to create in him the new humanity, that there is a new and righteous life in which we can share. The *action* of Christ on the cross is done and done well. It is finished and finished completely. Nevertheless, the *attitude* of Christ on the cross – his giving of himself in obedient response – is replicated in us because it was the basis of his earthly life and remains the basis of his heavenly existence. He gives himself to the Father because he loves the Father and this love is built to last for ever and to share with all.

Nevertheless, it needs to be recognized that the attitude of Christ is never fully reproduced in our worship. Our praise is always marked by penitence because it is always marred by sin. It remains in need of Christ's perfecting touch. I am not much of a singer. I find it difficult to stay in tune. But when I stand next to someone with a fine voice I find it much easier. The voice I hear in my ear helps to keep my voice on line and I like to think of my voice merging with that voice so that the faltering poverty of mine is purified and beautified by the richness of the other. This is a crude and very inadequate reflection of what happens when we worship. The integrity of the worship which comes from our lips and our hearts is retained – it remains our worship – but it is retuned by the greater integrity of the worship of Christ. The Spirit lifts our prayer and praise into the sphere of Christ's worship to be purified and perfected by his prayer and praise and then presented by Christ to the Father in its new and redeemed form. Our worship is *with* Christ our brother, *in* Christ our priest but always *through* Christ our sacrifice, whose death once for us is the means of our cleansing, renewing and perfecting.

We have talked a great deal about giving – the self-giving of the Son to the Father embodied in Jesus and replicated in us. But there is receiving as well as giving in God. The Son receives Sonship from the Father. The Spirit receives Spirithood from the Father. The Father receives Fatherhood from the Son's acceptance of Sonship. 'The persons', as Colin Gunton explains, 'are what they are by virtue of what they give to and receive from each other.'[22] This eternal giving and receiving between Father, Son and Spirit not only makes them what they are, it makes God who God is. Gunton goes on to say, 'as such they constitute the being of God, for there is no being of God underlying what the persons are to and from each other'.[23] God is an unimaginably joyful exchange of love in which each person delights in the other.

We shall look further at this mutual indwelling in love (*perichoresis* – to give it its technical term) in the next chapter. At this point we should simply register three implications for our worship which will need to be developed there. The first is that as well as inviting us into his giving of love and praise and worship *to* the Father, Christ also invites us into his receiving *from* the Father. The Report on *The Mystery of Salvation* by the Doctrine Commission of the Church of England describes the framework which a person needs to have in place before there can be any understanding of the Christian doctrine of salvation. It says, 'I do not know what Christians mean by salvation until I realise I can be fully myself only in receiving myself from God and in giving myself utterly to God'.[24] The same applies to our worship (because it is the experience of salvation): we can never know what Christians mean by worship until we realize that we can be fully ourselves only in receiving ourselves from God and in giving ourselves to God. The eternal Son is who he is because he receives being through the Spirit from the Father. Jesus is who he is because the eternal Son receives life and love through the Spirit from the Father in the full conditions of human existence. We can be what we are meant to be only as we share in his capacity to receive all that God has to give.

The second is that because God is eternally receiving as Father, Son and Spirit, as well as eternally giving, there is the ground in the being of God for his reception of our worship. Although God is perfect in himself and does not need to receive anything from anyone beyond himself, the action of receiving is not alien to him because he is eternally receiving as Father, Son and Spirit. God is Father, Son and Holy Spirit and Father, Son and Spirit are who they are because of all they receive from each other. This is how they are in their otherness from each other: they receive freedom to be what they are from each other. This is how they are in their togetherness with each other: they are bound to each other in reciprocal love.

The third point is that as our worship is communion with the Son and the Father in the Spirit and because we worship the God whose being is the communion of Father, Son and Holy Spirit, worship cannot be something we do independently of others. Father, Son and Spirit are not isolated individuals doing their own thing. They are persons who are what they are because they are related to the other. They call us out of individualism to personhood to discover who we are through our relationship with God and through our relationships with each other and with God's whole creation. The God whose being is a communion of love requires that those who come to worship him come prepared to take their place in the community of the Church and in the community of creation of which Christ is the head.

III A LITURGICAL EXAMPLE: THE INVITATION TO THE LORD'S SUPPER

The Invitation

Come ye hither all, whose taste
    Is your waste;
Save your cost, and mend your fare.
God is here prepared and dressed,
    And the feast,
God, in whom all dainties are.

Come ye hither all, whom wine
    Doth define,
Naming you not to your good:
Weep what ye have drunk amiss,
    And drink this,
Which before ye drink is blood.

Come ye hither all, whom pain
    Doth arraign,
Bringing all your sins to sight:
Taste and fear not: God is here
    In this cheer,
And on sin doth cast the fright.

Come ye hither all, whom joy
    Doth destroy,
While ye graze without your bounds:
Here is joy that drowneth quite
    Your delight,
As a flood the lower grounds.

Come ye hither all, whose love
    Is your dove,
And exalts you to the sky:
Here is love, which having breath
    Ev'n in death,
After death can never die.

Lord I have invited all,
    And I shall
Still invite, still call to thee:
For it seems but just and right
    In my sight,
Where is all, there all should be.[25]

I can remember being very moved many years ago by a poster of a simple loaf of bread, a glass of wine and words which ran something like this: 'Jesus of Nazareth requests your company at a meal to be held in his honour'. A poem by a seventeenth-century Anglican priest and a twentieth-century Christian advertising agency: different contexts and different Christian communities united in the common experience of knowing the one who graciously invites us to share his supper and his life.

It is in Luke's Gospel that Jesus' sense of joy at our company is conveyed most clearly. All the careful preparations have been made. The room is ready. The food and drink stand on the table. The people have arrived. As Jesus sits at his place he says to the disciples, '*I have eagerly desired to eat this Passover with you before I suffer*' (22:15). He has been longing for this moment to come, this chance to celebrate the Passover with his friends. Luke is the only Gospel writer to include the dominical instruction to 'Do this in remembrance of me'. The Jesus who has been waiting to eat and drink with his disciples takes the Passover bread and wine, gives them new meaning in the context of his coming death, offers them to his disciples and invites them to go on doing what he has just done in order to remember him.

In the Emmaus resurrection story, Luke shows what Jesus meant by the invitation to remember him in the celebration of his Supper. The Emmaus narrative progresses through three stages. As the disappointed disciples talk about the last few confusing days, Jesus draws alongside them. Unrecognized, he walks with them as a stranger. He simply asks some questions and then listens as they talk. He meets them *where they are*, with 'faces downcast' (24:17). In the next stage of the story he begins to speak. He takes them to the Scriptures and shows them the suffering of the Messiah. They begin to piece together the broken jigsaw of their hope. He meets them *in the word* and their 'hearts burn' (24:32). His words make them want him to stay with them. The story moves into its third stage. Here Jesus joins them for their supper. But he who is always host takes, blesses, breaks and gives them the bread they have provided. He meets them *at the table*, and their 'eyes are opened' (24:31). The story ends with them going to tell others that Christ is alive.

The three stages of Luke's narrative form the three structures of most revised liturgies of the Eucharist: Preparation, Word and Sacrament. I want briefly to look at each of these from the perspective of Jesus' invitation to us.

Preparation

Here Christ invites us to prepare ourselves to meet with him in word and sacrament. He meets us *where we are* (in our doubts and disappointments as well as in our hopes and joys) to lead us to *where he is* (in his place before the Father). Usually the liturgy begins with a greeting such as 'The Lord is here' or 'The Lord be with you' (which can also be rendered, from its Latin original, 'The Lord is with you'). We are being asked to welcome him as the *agent* of our worship. Other, more explicitly trinitarian greetings, invite us to make the love of the trinitarian God the *basis* of our worship. Several Christian traditions include a prayer (known as the Collect for Purity) near the beginning of their eucharistic worship which invites God to inspire our worship by the work of his Spirit. The Holy Spirit is welcomed as the *enabler* of our worship. A period of penitence follows in which we are invited to confess our sin and to receive God's forgiveness. Praise then takes over in the words of the *Gloria* as we join in a song, inspired by the cry of the angels at the birth of Jesus, which for fifteen hundred years has been sung in the Eucharist. The preparation is concluded by a collect. The collect should follow a time of silence for personal prayer and so function as an invitation to the people to gather their own prayers (collect them, as it were) into a common prayer for the day and week.

Word

Here we are invited to hear the story of our faith and respond to its call. God's word is ministered to us through Scripture and sermon. If the lectionary and the preacher are doing their jobs properly, week by week we should encounter God's glory revealed in Christ, made known in our midst through the power of the Spirit. We should be like Cleopas and his friend on the way to Emmaus, listening

167

to the story of God's dealings with his people and dis-
covering its centre in the dying and rising of Christ.

Robert Browning wrote a long and intriguing poem in
the form of a letter from Karshish, 'an Arab Physician', to
his friend Abib. Karshish tells how a journey has taken him
to Bethany where he meets a Jew called Lazarus. Lazarus is
an old man, thought to be mad. He tells Karshish a story
which seems both incredible and yet convincing. He says he
was brought back from death to life by a Nazarene sage.
What is more,

> This man so cured regards the curer, then,
> As – God forgive me! Who but God himself.

The poem ends with Karshish saying to Abib:

> The very God! think, Abib; dost thou think?
> So, the All-Great, were the All-Loving too –
> So, through the thunder comes a human voice
> Saying, 'O heart I made, a heart beats here!
> Face, my hands fashioned, see it in myself!
> Thou hast no power nor mayst conceive of mine,
> But love I gave thee, with myself to love,
> And thou must love me who have died for thee!'
> The madman saith He said so: it is strange.[26]

This is the word we need to hear again and again through
Scripture and sermon. Like Karshish we need to have our
preconceptions of God shattered and our conceptions
defined by God's own revelation of himself in Christ. But
unlike Karshish who walks away from the story muttering 'it
is strange', we are not to treat the story of our salvation
simply as an interesting intellectual idea. We are called to
respond to its truth, to step into the story.

In fact the rest of the Eucharist is a series of opportunities
to respond. In the Creed we own the story as it has been
summarized by the Church. We identify ourselves as

members of the Catholic – the universal – Church which believes in this way about God. We renew our faith in *the Almighty* and in *the only Son of God* and in *the Lord and giver of Life*. In the prayers we accept the invitation to join in Christ's intercession for the Church and the world. This can make prayer sound somewhat passive – as if it is simply acquiescing in Christ's perfect knowledge of the will of God. But we know that Christ's earthly prayer was full of passion. He prayed 'with loud cries and tears' (Heb. 5:7). If our prayer is to be modelled on his prayer it will also be the prayer of struggle which, as P.T. Forsyth liked to say, demands all the strength of our humanity.[27] Prayer involves the battle of fighting for what is right against all the principalities and powers, calling on God, as the Litany puts it, 'to finally beat down Satan under our feet'. Prayer involves the pain of seeing the gap between the kingdom of this world and the kingdom of God and the labour pain of being part of the kingdom's birth on earth. Paul claimed that the 'sighs too deep for words' (Rom. 8:26) in the prayer of the Church are in fact signs of the intercession of the Spirit in the life of the Church. This allows us to say that Christian prayer shares in the pain of the Spirit who yearns for the completion of God's purposes for the world. It also allows us to say that the prayer of the heavenly Christ remains a prayer of longing as well as a prayer of trust. The Spirit who groans within us is his Spirit. He too prays for the coming of the kingdom (Rom. 8:34). He is the priest who has borne the pain of the world and still bears its marks upon his body. He prays for the coming of the salvation for which he sacrificed himself (Heb. 7:25). He intercedes for the implementation of his victory over evil. Until the future manifestation of his kingdom and power and glory at his *parousia*, his prayer involves pain for the present anguish of the world. Christian prayer shares in the pain of his prayer as well as in his unmovable confidence in his victory.

Sacrament

For Anglicans the Ministry of the Sacrament usually begins with the sharing of the peace. In this position it is like a public and symbolic expression of the call in the (1662) *Book of Common Prayer* to 'Draw near with faith . . . and take this holy Sacrament' only if you are 'in love and charity with your neighbours'. We have heard the word of God inviting us to believe that God is the God of trinitarian and incarnational love. The implications of this faith for our Church and world have motivated our prayer. Now we are invited to demonstrate that we are prepared to live in that love. We are asked to greet each other in peace, to acknowledge that we belong together in one body and to affirm that we are bound by a common life.

It is then time to accept Jesus' invitation to 'Do this'. But what are we to do? How are we to fulfil Jesus' command? The stranger on the way to Emmaus was recognized as the risen Christ when he took the bread, gave thanks, broke the bread and gave it to his disciples. These were familiar actions. Jesus had done this when he fed the five thousand and when he shared the Passover with his disciples. He had probably done the same countless times at the many meals he ate with his friends. They are known as the fourfold action of the Eucharist. When liturgists from across the denominations were revising their eucharistic rites in the 1960s and 1970s they were determined to recover this simple, biblical structure which had become somewhat obscured over the preceding centuries. Most modern liturgies (including the new waves of revision in the 1990s) of whatever tradition in the western Church seek to make clear that Jesus has invited us to take bread and wine, to give thanks to God, to break the bread and then to give the bread and wine to be eaten and drunk.[28] By doing this we do as Jesus commanded. With the help of George Herbert's poetry I want to touch upon each of them.

WE ARE INVITED TO TAKE:

> Not in rich furniture, or fine array,
> Nor in a wedge of gold,
> Thou, who from me wast sold,
> To me dost now thyself convey.[29]

We take bread and wine, common things of life to 'set them apart', as Anglicans and Puritans liked to say in the seventeenth century, 'for a holy and godly use'.[30] There is a consistency here with all that the word should have told us earlier. God takes the ordinary things of earthly life to display the extraordinary glory of divine life.

WE ARE INVITED TO GIVE THANKS:

> What is this strange and uncouth thing?
> To make me sigh, and seek, and faint, and die,
> Until I had some place, where I might sing,
>   And serve thee; and not only I,
> But all my wealth, and family might combine
> To set thy honour up, as our design.[31]

In the eucharistic (thanksgiving) prayer we offer thanks and praise for God's goodness towards us in the whole sweep of salvation from the beginning of creation to the final coming of the kingdom but, with all the talk of body broken and blood shed, we cannot fail to focus on 'this strange and uncouth thing' of the cross. The movement of our thanks is *to* the Father (who gave his Son for us), *through* the Son (whose obedience to the Father took him to death for us) and *in* the Spirit (through whom the Son offered himself to the Father). As we have often said, our movement of praise is grounded in and is a participation in the eternal trinitarian movement of God which is embodied in the person of Jesus and exemplified in his work on the cross.

In chapter 4 we saw how Basil argued that there are two authentic patterns of Christian doxology. One gives glory to the Father through the Son in the Spirit. The other gives glory to the Father and the Son and the Holy Spirit. The eucharistic prayer offers an example of how the two can be brought together in Christian praise. We enter into the Father's presence to praise him by taking our place in the life of his Son through the Spirit who unites us to Christ. As we stand with Christ in his place before the Father we see the glory he has had with the Father 'before the foundation of the world' (John 17:24) and we see the glory of the Spirit who belongs to both the Father and the Son and yet remains distinct from them. From this place we perceive the glory of God's triune life and, recasting an ancient piece of Jewish liturgy, we sing 'Holy, holy, holy Lord, God of power and might'. The threefold repetition in Jewish worship served to acknowledge the perfection of God's holiness. In Christian worship it is used to ascribe perfection of divine holiness to the Father, and the Son and the Spirit, who *together* are one God, sharing one Lordship.[32] We then call upon the Spirit to act among us with holy and life-giving power and we acclaim Christ whose dying has destroyed our death and whose rising has restored our life. Within the triune life of God we, as it were, move around the Trinity glorifying Father, Son and Holy Spirit.

WE ARE INVITED TO BREAK THE BREAD:

> But as Pomanders and wood
> > Still are good,
> Yet being bruised are better scented:
> God, to show how far his love
> > Could improve,
> Here, as broken, is presented.[33]

The breaking of the bread (and the pouring of the wine) played a great part in seventeenth-century Puritan liturgy. Richard Baxter's *Reformed Liturgy* had these words at the fraction and libation:

> The body of Christ was broken for us, and offered once for all to sanctify us: behold the sacrificed Lamb of God that taketh away the sin of the world.
> We were redeemed in the precious blood of Christ, as of a lamb without blemish or spot.[34]

In modern rites the dramatic impact of the breaking of the bread illustrates not only the breaking of the body of Christ on the cross but also the nature of Christ's body in the Church. The many pieces of the broken bread belong to one loaf. In the breaking of the bread we are invited to behold the Christ who died for us and to see that we belong to each other because we all belong to the one body of Christ.

WE ARE INVITED TO RECEIVE:

> You must sit down, says Love, and taste my meat:
>   So I did sit and eat.[35]

Alasdair Heron offers this paraphrase of Jesus' invitation to eat his body and drink his blood:

> 'This is myself, whom God will give up for the sake of all . . .
> This is myself, and in me the promise of the Father. Take it, drink it, and receive your own place in the covenant I will make, the covenant which I am.'[36]

Thomas Smail has a similar but simpler version: 'This is me for you'.[37] Jesus comes to us through bread and wine. All we have to do is to open our hearts as we open our hands and welcome his coming.

The final invitation of the Eucharist is a call to go out in the power of the Spirit and in the name of Christ to be God's people in God's world for God's glory. The Emmaus-bound former followers of a prophet were transformed into Jerusalem-bound witnesses to the risen Lord because they met him in the unfolding of the Scriptures and in the breaking of the bread. We too are sent back into the world to lead our lives in a new direction and to extend the invitation of Christ to all.

7

oooooooooo

The Searching of the Spirit

The Spirit is the breath from the mouth of God,
the one who announces the Word.
(John of Damascus[1])

I WHO IS THE SPIRIT?

As I write there is a storm raging outside. I knew that it was
coming. The wind was strong as I walked home. It buffeted
against me, blowing me this way and then that, at times
pushing me from behind and then pressing against me from
the front. It was invisible but irresistibly powerful. It was also
penetrating, reaching my body, as it hunted out every gap
in my clothing, and also my mind, as it seemed to clear away
the mental fog accumulated during the day. Even though it
had been hard work battling with the strength of the wind,
I arrived home refreshed and alert. I was able to think
more clearly and to see all sorts of issues and concerns more
accurately. Wind does have the power to reveal, to show
things as they really are. When it blows against a building it
reveals whether it is stable. When it blows against a person
it reveals whether their clothing is warm enough. When it
blows against a yacht, it reveals whether the crew are able to
harness its strength.

God is like the wind. He works invisibly but immensely
powerfully and he reveals truthfully and faithfully. This is
why the Hebrew word for God's Spirit is *ruach*, which has

the root meaning of 'wind'. When the Old Testament talks of God's *ruach*, his Spirit, it refers to God's powerful action and his faithful revelation.[2] It is this revealing work of the Spirit which we shall concentrate on in this chapter – the Spirit's ability to clear away the debris from the littered landscapes of our ordinary perceptions and to show us how things truly are in the extraordinary life of God. To help us to do this we turn to one of Paul's most important expositions of the identity and activity of the Spirit of God. He is writing to the Corinthian church, a Christian community familiar with the presence of the Spirit but also in danger of devaluing the demanding intellectual and ethical task to which the Spirit calls us, by which the mind of Christ (1 Cor. 2:16, 14:14–15) and the love of Christ (1 Cor. 13) are formed within us.

Paul begins his first letter to the Corinthians by talking about 'the message of the cross' (1:18). He claims that although this message appears to be foolishness it is in fact the wisdom of God. He reminds them that when he first came to them he 'decided to know nothing . . . except Jesus Christ and him crucified' (2:2). He acknowledges that the story of a crucified human being seems an unlikely stage for the unveiling of the truth about God but he goes on to say:

> 'What no eye had seen, nor ear heard,
>   nor the human heart conceived,
> what God has prepared for those
>   who love him' –
> these things God has revealed to us through the Spirit; for the Spirit searches everything, even the depths of God. For what human being knows what is truly human except the human spirit that is within? So also no one comprehends what is truly God's except the Spirit of God. (1 Cor. 2:9–11)

Paul's words about the Spirit as the one who 'searches everything, even the depths of God' (2:10) were often quoted by the Fathers of the early centuries of the Church. Athanasius' own *Statement of Faith*, for example, put them into credal form: 'We believe, likewise, also in the Holy Spirit that searches all things, even the deep things of God, and we anathematise doctrines contrary to this'.[3] The orthodox Fathers took Paul's point seriously that only if the Spirit belongs to God can the Spirit reveal to us that which is of God. Just as our spirits belong to our essence, to the very depths of who we are, so God's Spirit belongs to his being and is found at the heart, the centre, the depth, of God's inner life. From this place in the depths of God the Spirit comes to us in our depths – 'deep calling to deep', as the psalm has it (42:7) – and reveals the mystery (the secret wisdom) of who God is, or rather, reveals to us the reality of who God has shown himself to be in the Christ who was crucified.

As we have seen earlier, it was impossible for Paul, and indeed the later Fathers, that this revelation should be inconsistent with the way God had shown himself to be in the history of Israel. Nevertheless, by its very nature as the eschatological revelation, the full and definitive manifestation of the identity of God had to be fuller and richer than all that had been known in the past. As the eschatological revelation it was transcendent over all that had gone before, so that although it would not contradict the way God had revealed himself to be, it would complete God's revelation in ways which were beyond human expectation.

We know from Paul's own life story that he did not expect the troublesome person of Jesus who had been recently and, so he would have thought, justifiably crucified, to have any positive religious significance. But on his way to Damascus and through his subsequent thinking, reading of the Jewish Scriptures, praying, worshipping and sharing in the life of the Christian community, the Spirit had shown him the truth that Christ is 'the Lord of glory' (2:8). Basil of Caesarea in the fourth century used the analogy of the Spirit as a kind of search light, lighting up or revealing Christ as the image of God through whom we come to know and meet with God. Without the light of the Spirit, Christ remains unidentified and God, ultimately, unknown.[4] This picture captures something of the dynamic of the New Testament experience. The Spirit shines on others rather than himself. The spotlight of his love falls on the Father and the Son to reveal the glory of who they are and it falls on the believers to reveal the glory into which they are being transformed (2 Cor. 3:18). The Spirit had revealed to Paul that the Jesus whom he was persecuting was in fact the bearer of the divine name. The wisdom through which God had lovingly created the world and through which he continued to relate to the world had become embodied in the world to suffer for the world. This was the light which Paul had seen the Spirit shine upon the Son and which had revealed to him the significance of Jesus to the life of God. In this way the Spirit is self-effacing. He points to the face of the Father revealed in the face of the Son. Nevertheless, even though the Spirit directs the light of revelation away from himself, the same light is inevitably reflected back upon him because he is the one in whom the Father and the Son are known and loved. Hence although Paul does not focus on the distinctive identity of the Spirit in the way he does with the Son, it is clear that he sees the presence of the Spirit in his life and in the life of the Christian community as the personal presence of God dwelling amidst his people. Later, Gregory of Nazianzus was to claim that by being 'resident and active' in the Church the Spirit had 'demonstrated himself' and led the Church into the knowledge of his divinity.[5]

The role of the Spirit as the one who comes from God to bring us into a true understanding of God is given a prominent place in the *Pentecostarion*, the Eastern Orthodox liturgies of the Feast of Pentecost. In the liturgies the new tongues which are given to the apostles represent the gift of divine knowledge. They are signs of the Church's initiation into the language of God. The apostles do not just communicate with people of different languages, they speak to them of the deep things of God communicated to them by God.

The ancient liturgies of Eastern Orthodoxy would agree with J.H. King, one of the early leaders of the Pentecostal Movement of this century, who believed that, at its most profound level, the outpouring of the Spirit on the Day of Pentecost was a revelation of the Trinity. He was convinced of this because he and others had discovered, through their overwhelming experiences of the Spirit in their personal pentecosts, an intensifying of their love of the Father and the Son *and* a deep awareness of the interpenetrative unity of Father, Son and Spirit.[6] Our task in the rest of this chapter is to look more closely at this work of the *searching Spirit* in order to explore more of what he reveals about the trinitarian life of God and to consider, in the light of this, his role in our worship of the trinitarian God.

II PERSPECTIVES ON THE SPIRIT

The Spirit and fellowship

The Spirit who reveals the deep things of God reveals the fellowship which the Son has with the Father and which he has with them as the Spirit of the Father and the Son. He shows that God's life is a life of fellowship, that God's being is, in John Zizioulas' phrase, *being as communion*. Moreover, the Spirit is the one in whom they have their fellowship. The Spirit is shared by them – they have him in common. Hence the Spirit is the basis of their common life. In the Spirit they are one. And yet although the Spirit binds Father and Son together as one, he also preserves their distinctiveness. As

179

the *Father's* Spirit he is the gift of the Father's fellowship to the Son and as the *Son's* Spirit he is the gift of the Son's fellowship to the Father. All the time the Spirit remains distinct as himself – a divine person of equal honour and glory as the Father and the Son. As well as being the gift of fellowship between Father and Son the Spirit is the giver of his own fellowship to them. In this way the Spirit is like a child through whom a mother and father love each other and by whom they are held together in fellowship but who remains distinct from them and gives to them his own love of them and so has fellowship with them.

The fellowship of the Holy Spirit is given to us by the love of God and the grace of our Lord Jesus Christ (2 Cor. 12:13). The Spirit in whom Father and Son have fellowship is given to us so that in their Spirit we might share in their fellowship. God's eternal life of love has entered human history in the person of Jesus by the power of the Spirit and this same Spirit now extends to us the hand of fellowship and offers to give us a new birth into the life of Christ. The humanity of Christ into which we are initiated by the Spirit has been so renewed and reconstituted by the Spirit that it is committed to a life of fellowship. Hence, to experience eschatological salvation means not only to be drawn into the life of God's fellowship but to be driven into fellowship with God's people. The new believers on the day on which the Spirit was first poured out on all flesh '*devoted themselves* to . . . the fellowship' (Acts 2:42). In the new community created by the Spirit the walls of racial hostility, sexual discrimination and social convention were broken down as Jew and Gentile, male and female, free and slave were welded together into one worshipping body. The forming of fellowship has always been a sign of the Spirit's work. It was said in the days of the Azusa Street revival at the beginning of the century that the clearest evidence of it being an authentically pentecostal work of God was not that people spoke in tongues but that 'the color line was washed away in the blood'.[7] For a short time at least black and white stood together in the unity of the Spirit. The work of the eschatological Spirit is to bring about the eschatological community – to realize in the present something of the future life of God's people, when all our relationships will be perfected in the kingdom of righteousness.

Because Christian existence is necessarily communal, so is its defining activity of worship. In fact, it is in the context of his teaching about worship that Paul develops his analogy of the Church as the body of Christ. Each member of the Church is like a different part of a body, uniquely gifted by the Spirit for the common good. Paul's picture of the Church in 1 Corinthians 12–14 looks like an image of Trinity. The distinct identity and role of each person is defined through a complex web of interrelationships. Just as the eye can only be an eye by being connected to the ears and feet and hands, so the one who prophesies can only do so in so far as he or she is enabled and supported by those with wisdom and knowledge and the discernment of spirits.

From the perichoretic pattern of the Spirit's work in the charismatic worship of the Pauline churches we can see various orders or offices of ministry developing – prophets, teachers, leaders and others. The Spirit is active in every member of the Church searching out those gifts with which they have been created and supplying the new gifts of the kingdom with which God graciously equips his people for worship and witness. The Spirit of life both creates this rich diversity of spiritual life and brings it into the order of one interdependent whole. The Spirit, in Michael Welker's words, 'connects intense experiences of individuality with a new experience of community'.[8] He does this not just within a particular congregation but between congregations. In traditional catholic order this takes the form of many communities held together in one diocese by one bishop but it is a propensity of the Spirit that goes beyond the ecclesiastical systems of our divided Church. The worshipping people of Christ in every denomination and every nation and every culture are related to each other in one common life of the Spirit. Indeed, their fellowship extends even beyond the divide of death to the communion of saints – the life of shared worship which all those who are in Christ enjoy through the fellowship of the Holy Spirit.

The Spirit and the humanity of Christ

The fellowship which the Spirit gives us with the life of God is through the humanity of Christ. The fundamental insight of Christian faith from its earliest stage has been that 'Christ belongs to God' (1 Cor. 3:23). We have seen how the New Testament writers made use of motifs such as the wisdom and word of God which were part of the theological culture of Jewish thought to make sense of their convictions about Jesus without betraying the values of their Jewish monotheism. These helped them to say that the God who had been always speaking to his people and acting for their good had been embodied in Jesus (Col. 1:19), that the Word had become flesh (John 1:14), that the Alpha and Omega of Hebrew faith was to be found in 'the living one' of Christian experience (Rev. 1:8, 18). We have also seen how in the centuries following the New Testament the Church struggled to discern and define the full implications of this for its understanding of God, eventually affirming that the Son is *homoousios* (of one being) with the Father and that the Son has become incarnate, by the power of the Spirit, in Jesus of Nazareth.

As Jesus, the eternal Son, remains God the incarnation does not involve an abandonment of deity. Neither does it involve the absorption of humanity into God. Rather it involves the adoption of humanity into the dynamics of the divine life. In Jesus, through the Spirit, the eternal Son includes the life of a human being in his life. In Jesus we have the divine life of the eternal Son lived out in human form. But what is the divine life of the eternal Son? How is the eternal Son God?

The eternal Son is God because he is begotten by the Father through and in the Spirit.[9] God is an eternal event of love in which the Father generates, begets, gives life and being to his Son through and in his Spirit – the expression or gift of his love. The Son eternally receives life and being and returns his love in the form of the same Spirit who is also the expression or gift of his love. This eternal dynamic of God's being is lived out by the Son in the conditions and constraints of human life. The essence of the Son's identity – the glory of his divinity as the Son of the Father begotten in the Spirit – becomes embodied in the humanity of Jesus. The eternal relationship between the Son and the Father in the Spirit takes on human form. We can see this most transparently in the prayer life of Jesus: 'At the same hour Jesus rejoiced in the Holy Spirit and said, "I thank you Father . . ." ' (Luke 10:21). Jesus prays in the Spirit to the Father.

We also see it in the ministry of Christ. Jesus does the Father's work of healing the sick and casting out demons by the power of the Spirit. Much of the traditional incarnational theology of the Church has implied that Jesus was able to perform miracles simply because he was God. In an attempt to correct the traditional tendency to ignore Jesus' humanity and bypass the work of the Spirit, some charismatic Christology implies that in his incarnate form the Son was forced to operate out of the Spirit's empowering because the power of his own divine being had been laid aside. While deserving credit for recovering the role of the Spirit in relation to the humanity of Christ, this view fails to recognize that the Son is eternally operating out of the

Spirit. The Son is eternally begotten by the Father in the Spirit. In the incarnation the Son does not become anything different from who he is in his essence – his relation to the Father in the Spirit remains the same. Rather, the Son's relation to the Father came to be lived out in the conditions of human existence. The incarnation does not involve God in contradictions. Although it is a different *place* to be God, the human life of Jesus does not involve a different *way* of being God because the basis of the Son's being, his relationship to the Father in the Spirit, is maintained in the Jesus who prays *Abba* in the Spirit.

All this means that when we are brought into communion with the humanity of Christ by the Spirit we are sharing in the real life of God. Our experience of God is not an adaptation of God to meet the limitation of our humanity, it is the gift of God's real self. When we preach and teach in the Spirit, when we praise and pray in the Spirit, when we receive gifts from God in the Spirit and minister in the Spirit, we are participating not just in the way the Son relates to God in his human form but in the eternal movements of the Son's giving to and receiving from the Father in the Spirit.

Assured that the incarnation is the incarnation of the way God is in himself we can now move on to consider the impact of the embodiment of the Son through the Spirit on the humanity assumed. Thomas Smail identifies three distinctive works of the Spirit on the humanity of Christ at three stages in Jesus' life.[10] The first is when Jesus is conceived by the power of the Holy Spirit. Jesus' humanity comes into existence by the direct action of God. This is a redemptive movement of the Spirit by which a new propensity to respond to God is breathed into human life. The propensity becomes a reality as Jesus struggles against temptation and fashions a sinless life. The second is at Jesus' baptism when the Spirit anoints him for messianic ministry.

The evidence that Jesus is the Messiah, the *Christos* – the anointed one – is his life of ministry in which people encounter the kingdom of God and in his death for the cause of the kingdom. The third is when Jesus is raised from the dead by the action of God through the Spirit and exalted to the right hand of God. The one who was born through the action of the Spirit and empowered by the Spirit is now 'vindicated by the Spirit' (1 Tim. 3:16). In these great eschatological acts the Spirit transfigures Christ into the reality of the new creation.

According to Peter's sermon on the Day of Pentecost the risen and exalted Christ, 'having received from the Father the promise of the Holy Spirit' (Acts 2:33), becomes the giver of the Spirit to all who believe. Through this Spirit we participate in Christ's redeemed, messianic and eschatological humanity. The Spirit regenerates us. The Spirit empowers us. The Spirit transfigures us. All that the Spirit has completed in Christ is applied to us. We are born from above, anointed for service and transformed into new creatures.

This work of the Spirit on our humanity is rooted in the worshipping life of the Church. There are at least three reasons for this. First, the new humanity of Christ, in which we share by the Spirit, is doxological by nature. He gives glory to the Father in the Spirit. To enter the realm of Christ's humanity is to step into a life of worship. Second, as we said earlier, the new humanity of Christ is relational by nature. Sharing in Christ's humanity through the fellowship of the Spirit means sharing in the life of his people and sharing in the life of Christ's people means sharing in their life of worship. Third, the actions of the Spirit on our humanity are signified in the liturgical actions of the Church. The regenerating work of the Spirit is signified in baptism, the empowering in confirmation and the transfiguring in the Eucharist. In the language of the Church of

England's Thirty-nine Articles these are *effectual signs* – they effect what they signify. In baptism we are given new life. In confirmation we are empowered. In the Eucharist we are transformed into the likeness of Christ. And yet this can only happen in as much as we (again following the Articles) *rightly receive* what is given.[11] God has revealed himself to be in essence relational, therefore God's action upon us always takes place in relational terms. The Spirit not only sanctifies the signs so that they become tools in the purposes of God, he opens our eyes to see their significance and opens our hearts to receive the work which God does through him. The new humanity which the Spirit formed in Christ is *responsive* – it is open to God. The Spirit draws us into this responsiveness of Christ and forms within us the same willingness to say 'yes' to God.

All this means that at the heart of worship should be what liturgists call the *epiclesis* – the petition for the coming of the Holy Spirit. The Church is, in the words of the Anglican-Orthodox Dialogue, 'that Community which lives by continually invoking the Holy Spirit'.[12] Our worship, like every other aspect of our common life, is dependent on the one who comes to search us out in our old humanity to take us deeper into the humanity of Christ. Not only on Pentecost Sunday but at every moment the cry of the Church is:

> Come, Holy Ghost, our souls inspire,
> and lighten with celestial fire;
> Thou the anointing Spirit art,
> who dost thy sevenfold gifts impart.[13]

The Spirit and the future

On a number of occasions we have referred to how in Jewish and Christian thought the Spirit was conceived of as the eschatological Spirit – the Spirit of God's future reign. The Spirit would anoint God's servant to proclaim God's kingdom of liberation, healing and justice (Isa. 61:1–4). The Spirit would be poured out on all people regardless of age, sex, race and social standing (Joel 2:28–9). By the time of the New Testament period most Jewish traditions believed that the life-giving work of the Spirit at the fulfilment of God's purposes would bring about the resurrection of the dead. The early Christians were convinced that the longed-for events had begun in Jesus. He was the anointed one by whom people were set free, healed and restored to fellowship with God and each other. Jesus had been raised from the dead. He was the first fruit of the coming resurrection (1 Cor. 15:20). The Spirit had been poured out on his people. The conditions of God's future reign were present in the life of the Church and most noticeably in its worship as the believers broke bread 'with jubilation' (Acts 2:46), experiencing the unbounded joy of God's kingdom. They knew of course that there was more of the kingdom to come and that God's purposes were still to be completely fulfilled, but they knew that still they stood within the *real presence* of the kingdom. Just as in the commercial world of the time an *arrabōn* (down payment) was given as a first instalment of the total payment, the Spirit had been given as the *arrabōn* of God's future reign. The Spirit was, in Gordon Fee's words, 'the *certain evidence* that the future had dawned, and the *absolute guarantee* of its final consummation'.[14]

This understanding of the Spirit as the Spirit of God's future reign who breaks into our lives, our worship and our world with the new life of God's kingdom should warn against tendencies to domesticate the Spirit. It is all too easy to see the Spirit as the possession of the Church or even of the world rather than the gift of God. Yes, the Spirit is the creator Spirit by whom God has constant connection with his creation. Yes, the Spirit is the Spirit of the Church's fellowship by whom God activates all its life. But the Spirit is primarily the *Holy* Spirit who comes from the holiness of

God and his kingdom as breath, wind and fire to transform our world and worship into the ways and will of God. Even as the Creator Spirit the Spirit is transcendent to the creation – including the Church – and not trapped within either. He comes in the transcendent freedom of God to confront us with the realities of God's kingdom and to create in us the freedom to respond to God and to live in the way of his kingdom.

As the Spirit inspires our worship we become conscious that we are participating in our eschatological salvation. Here and now we are tasting 'the powers of the age to come' (Heb. 6:4) and sharing in the marriage feast of the Lamb (Rev. 19:9). This means that it should be quite normal to expect to see signs of the presence of that future kingdom in our midst. However, as the Spirit inspires our worship we also become conscious of all that is not complete in the salvation of the world. The joy of the presence of the future is always tempered by the pain of the wait for its fullness. The Church may anticipate the food and drink of the kingdom but it also cries 'Come, Lord Jesus' and so finds its worship not a flight into otherworldly escapism but an empowering to confront all that falls short of God's kingdom in the kingdom of this world. Steven Land describes how the tension between the already and not yet manifests itself in the worship of the Pentecostal tradition: 'Pentecostals who are moved deeply and powerfully by the Spirit will laugh and cry, dance and wait in stillness. In the Spirit they "already" participate in the marriage supper but also live in the "not yet" of a lost world.'[15] This relationship between present reality and future hope is of the essence of Christian worship because it is of the essence of Christian salvation. We know that the kingdom is here because God is so close that he can be called *Abba*, and yet when we pray '*Abba*, Father' we ask for the kingdom to come.[16]

The kingdom which the Spirit brings is the new creation inaugurated in Christ. God has acted by his Spirit on the body of Christ to recreate it into the eschatological form of the new creation. In the Spirit we yearn for the same action of God upon our material existence, 'the redemption of our bodies' (Rom. 8:23). Because Christian worship is an anticipation of the new creation it necessarily involves our material existence. In fact, because we are embodied beings it cannot be otherwise. As far as we are concerned there is no purely spiritual activity. Every action, emotion and affection is a complex interplay between our bodies, minds and spirits. But God's action upon our materiality is not a concession to our present state, it is dictated by God's future purposes for us. Our worship involves the physicality of our bodies and other aspects of our material existence because we will remain embodied beings taking our place in a renewed creation. From the electrical impulses of our brains to the bending of our knees our bodies are engaged in the experience of worship both as receivers of the Spirit's work upon us and as transmitters of the worship the Spirit inspires in us. The Spirit's material work in our worship also extends to other elements of our creation. Bread and wine, oil and light, art and sound are sanctified by God's Holy Spirit and so are transfigured into signs and gifts of the new creation.

III THE EVENT OF WORSHIP

Worship is an event. It is rooted in the event of God. God's being is an eternal event in which the Father eternally gives glory to the Son in the Spirit and the Son eternally gives glory to the Father in the Spirit. This is how God is God. Christian worship is a participation in this eventful life of God through the presence and activity of the Holy Spirit in the life of the believer and in the midst of the fellowship of the Church. John Zizioulas describes how the Church is both *instituted by Christ* and *constituted by the Spirit*.[17] I once asked Archbishop Gregorios, the Greek Orthodox Archbishop of Thyateira and Great Britain, about this idea of the Church being constituted – brought about as a contemporary reality – by the work of the Spirit, wondering whether it was simply a perspective of one particular theologian. The enthusiasm of his response convinced me that this is a pervading understanding of the Church and the nature of its worship in Eastern Orthodox theology. He pointed me to the hymns of the Festival of Pentecost as a sample of Orthodoxy's implicit recognition that the Church's life is perpetually dependent on the present working of the Spirit. Although Zizioulas is critical of the western theological tradition for concentrating too heavily on the historical continuity with Christ's institution of the Church – whether through popes in succession to Peter or teaching in line with Paul – there are various indications that western theology is recovering a proper emphasis on the Spirit as the enabler and activator of the Church's life and worship, some of which we have drawn upon already.

Paul built his theology on the conviction that the eschatological promises were being fulfilled and that God had come to dwell with his people. The believer and the fellowship of believers have become the temple of the Holy Spirit. The Spirit is the gift of God which brings the Church – the company of those who have entered into the eschatological life of heirdom to God – into being. 'Where the Church is, there also is the Spirit of God; and where the Spirit of God is, there is the Church' as Irenaeus said.[18] Nevertheless, although by definition the Spirit is present wherever there is Christian faith and life, the Spirit does not belong to the Church. The Spirit remains the *given* not the *owned*, always in the realm of promise, not possession. This has to be the case because the Spirit initiates us into the relational life of God where the interaction of Father, Son and Spirit is grounded in freedom. The Son freely enters into all that the Father gives to him in the Spirit and freely gives all that he has to give to the Father in the Spirit.

It is the same for the Church as it lives in the life of Christ. All that God gives to us by the Spirit needs to be welcomed and received in an ongoing way. The confidence that God has given the Spirit to the Church should not lead us to complacent assurance that authentic worship will automatically happen simply by virtue of the fact that we are the Church. It should compel us to enter more deeply into the gift God has given so that our worship can be truly inspired by virtue of the fact that the Spirit is breaking us out of our preoccupation with ourselves and taking us into the love which Christ has for God. In the rest of this chapter I want to focus on two aspects of our worship and reflect on the part the Spirit plays in them.

'The Word of the Lord': God's word to us

We have implied on a number of occasions that the event of worship is not just about what we give to God but what God gives to us. A good proportion of any event of worship involves the ministry of God's word to us in a number of ways. One of these is the reading of the Scriptures. The Spirit has an intrinsic relationship to the Bible. The Scriptures are inspired by the Spirit – their cause is the breath of God upon his people (2 Tim. 3:16). The events they record and the experiences to which they refer are the results of the Spirit's activity. The interpretation of those events and experiences were guided by the Spirit. The criteria by which the books of the Bible were accepted as Holy Scripture and drawn together in a canon of Scripture were defined by the Spirit witnessing to their truth in the life of the communities in which they were read (1 John 2:26–7).

191

Just as their cause is God's breath so is their effect. The Spirit enables the words of Scripture to be heard as God's word today. Extending Basil's image of the Spirit as a search light exposing God's truth, we can say that the Spirit does this by shining his light both on the ancient Scriptures of the Church and on the contemporary situation of the Church in order to bring the one to bear on the other, to allow us – in the words of a familiar prayer – to hear, mark and inwardly digest what God is saying to the Church and the world.

As well as speaking God's word through the reading of Scripture, the Spirit also speaks through the teaching ministries of the Church which in different ways apply scriptural truth and guide people in service to the God of Scripture. Here again the Spirit's work has two aspects which are brought together in one result. The Spirit both searches out the catholic truth of the Church and the contemporary context of the Church in order to reveal what it means to live as Christians in the present. This involves both proclaiming and prophesying. The deep things of God which the Spirit has revealed to the Church in Christ need to be affirmed and reaffirmed in a thorough proclamation of the good news of God. The liturgical year, as it moves through the great doctrines of the faith, disciplines the Church to grapple with the great claims of Christian theology. The Spirit enables God's people to recall Christ's words and ways and to enter into a deeper understanding of their significance (John 14:25, 16:12–15). All this of course is not simply for our erudition. It is to form Christ within us. It is to take us further into the life of worship which he lives before the Father.

Together with the proclamatory work of the Spirit there is the prophetic work of the Spirit, by which I mean the application of the deep things of God to the particular contexts in which we find ourselves. The Puritan preachers of the seventeenth century discovered the power of inspired preaching. Groups of them would meet for 'prophesying meetings' which were a cross between a sermon class and a Bible study. They would share views on biblical passages and listen to each other preach, working together to see how God's word related both to matters of personal piety and the current needs of the Church. The great strength of Puritan preaching was its belief that God does speak into the particularities of our personal and corporate experience. As a result Puritan congregations placed great expectations on the sermon as an opportunity not just to hear about God but to be addressed by God.

Another example of the prophetic work of the Spirit is speaking into the social and political realities of the time, relating the abiding message of the gospel to the particularities of political situations which are always changing. A host of Christian leaders who have been used by the Spirit to apply the liberating principles of the gospel to the situations of their time come to mind. Dietrich Bonhoeffer, Martin Luther King, Desmond Tutu and Lesslie Newbigin are four notable examples but there are many others ranging from bishops in the House of Lords in London, relating the gospel to the legislation of their nation, to pastors in Rwanda and Burundi, speaking of reconciliation in lands torn apart by racial hatred.

A third dimension of the prophetic work of the Spirit is emphasized in the Pentecostal and Charismatic traditions. Here God is expected to speak through words of wisdom and knowledge, pictures and visions, revealing his will for a whole range of very particular circumstances. These concern not only the quality of the worship and the needs of the worshippers, but also the congregation's calling to meet the needs of the world through all manner of acts of ministry and mission.

All three examples of the prophetic work of the Spirit – in which God's eternal word is particularized in the present context of our worship – should not be seen as the property of the individual traditions where they find a natural welcome. They belong to the whole Church as part of the ministry of the Spirit who takes what is Christ's and applies it to us.

As well as relating the proclaimed word of God to particular situations the Spirit also enacts the word in visible and concrete ways. Again different traditions have emphasized this aspect of the Spirit's work in different ways. The sixteenth-century Reformers emphasized how the word is sealed in the sacraments of baptism and holy communion. The word of God's gracious incorporation into the life of Christ is sealed in the action of baptism. The word of God's gracious gift of continuing fellowship with Christ and his benefits is sealed in the Eucharist. In the theology of the Reformers the sacraments are enactments – visible and tangible expressions – of the word. In various activist forms of Christian faith, such as the base communities of South America, the word is practised in action. The reflection of the Bible in the acts of worship is directed towards its implications for living. The worshippers will leave the worship determined to put the liberating word of the gospel into practice in the oppressive conditions of human life and will then report on how the word has been lived out and the difference it has made at a subsequent act of worship. Amongst Pentecostals and Charismatics the word is demonstrated in times of ministry in which the word of God's healing or forgiveness, renewal or challenge is expected to be confirmed by God's action amongst his people.

All three point to the same dynamic between word and Spirit which we have already observed. The Spirit takes the constant content of God's word of grace and realizes it in the changing conditions of our world. Just as the Spirit empowered Jesus so the Spirit goes on empowering God's word in Christ so that it performs what it proclaims. Again, none of these dimensions of the Spirit's activity should be seen as the possession of one particular tradition of the Church. They belong to the Spirit and therefore are available to the whole Church, though of course they will be contextualized in different ways in the different cultures of the Church.

'O Lord, open our lips': our response to God

It is only by means of the Spirit that we can respond to God in prayer and praise. Nevertheless, because the Spirit is the one who holds the Father and the Son in perichoretic unity in which their otherness is not subsumed in their togetherness, the Spirit always works through the integrity of our freedom. Tom Smail has a helpful way of expressing the nature of our response to God: 'we must indeed answer *for* ourselves, but we do not and cannot answer *by* ourselves'.[19] We can see this in Mary. She says her 'yes' to God and gives her praise to God but she does so because of the Spirit's work upon her bringing to her God's word of grace. It is the same with Paul. He confesses Jesus as his Lord and he prays to God as his *Abba*, but only because the Spirit has revealed Christ to him and drawn him into Christ's own prayer. Indeed, we see the same pattern at work in Jesus himself. His whole life is an act of worship to the Father because he has been born of the Spirit and anointed by the Spirit. In fact it is Christ's obedient self-giving to God through the Spirit, culminating in his giving on the cross, which constitutes the perfect human response to God into which Mary, Paul and every believer are brought into communion through the Spirit.

Because our prayer takes place through the enabling of the Spirit, it is stamped with eschatological characteristics. We pray as citizens of heaven, enjoying the privileges this brings, yet our prayer is for the establishment of the kingdom on earth and so we suffer the pain of waiting and willing for its coming. It is no accident that the only place in the Gospels where Jesus' *Abba* address to God is left untranslated is in his Gethsemane prayer. The sighs which he prayed then and which remain part of his prayer until the kingdom for which he died is finally and fully established, are replicated in us as we cry *Abba* and intercede with 'sighs too deep for words' (Rom. 8:26), sharing in the fellowship of Christ's suffering (Phil. 3:10). But as we have seen, the eschatological work of the Spirit also involves bringing God's future to bear on our present, not only by identifying the gap between what is and what is to come, but also by breaking God's future into our present in order to begin to close the gap. In our prayer the Spirit searches out those points and places in our present where God's future can be applied. This means that prayer involves listening to God's Spirit and working with him where he is bringing people and political situations, churches and communities into the conditions – even if only briefly and ever so provisionally – of God's kingdom.

Prayer also involves confession as well as intercession. Here we see the Spirit at work in the convicting role promised in Jesus' farewell sermons in John's Gospel. The Spirit searches out our sin and our part in the world's sin. The Spirit then reveals to us the forgiveness of God and begins to search out in us the attitude of Christ's obedience so that his perfection may be formed in us. John and Charles Wesley developed a doctrine which became known as 'sinless perfection'. It was a theology open to both misunderstanding and abuse but at its heart it was simply an attempt to express the genuine Christian experience of being so 'renewed in love',[20] so transformed and transfigured by the Spirit, that at least for a moment – perhaps a moment of repentance and absolution – one loses 'the love of sinning'.[21]

The Spirit leads us into praise as well as prayer. He gathers us into the love which the Son has for the Father. We said earlier that the Spirit is the expression of the Son's love for the Father – the outward movement of the Son in self-giving to the Father. This means that the Spirit not only relates us to Christ, he locates us in the Son's delight for the Father and in his joyous self-giving to the Father. We enter into the reciprocity between Father and Son and glorify the one in whom the Father is well pleased. At the same time we receive the pleasure which the Father has for the Son and we too are glorified. We are not glorified as God but we are glorified as human beings (John 17:22) in the sense that in Christ we reach the perfection for which God created us. God's image is restored within us and amongst us. Although essentially an eschatological reality which is still to be fully realized, the restoration of God's image in his people is anticipated when they praise.

The image of God in humanity must have a trinitarian form. It must be to do with unity in diversity into unity and with relationality. When we praise we are made more fully integrated as human beings. The diverse dimensions of all that makes us who we are are brought into a unity of focus upon God. Our bodies, minds and spirits are brought together into one whole as we offer with our whole being the sacrifice of praise. The restoration of a trinitarian image of God in the depths of individual lives as they contemplate God was a particular interest of Augustine. Although there are dangers in Augustine's tendency to see the most perfect forms of the image of God in the inner workings of the human mind, rather than in the offering of the whole self to God, his emphasis on the renewal of the image of God in each person is a wholly good one. Where it needs to be balanced is by giving proper place to the more Cappadocian emphasis on the relational character of the image of God and by recognizing the connection between the two. Christ is a fully integrated human being precisely because he is truly relational. It is as Jesus authentically relates to God, to those he encounters and to the environment in which he is placed, that the image of God is restored in him. Through the Spirit we are at one with Christ and offer praise to the Father. We do so in relation to all God's people. The Spirit draws us into the fellowship of the Church to take our place as members of one body. In our praise we are also related to the earth, both in the sense that we use the things of the earth – light, water, oil, bread and wine – and in the sense that our praise is the voice of an earth full of the glory of God. As we allow ourselves to become persons in relationship giving ourselves in love for the other, rather than isolated individuals seeking what is good for ourselves, the image of God within and between his people is restored. It is in praise that the greatest possibilities for this profound change can be formed.

CONCLUSION

8

The Trinity, Worship and Mission

The first missionary was God the Father, who sent forth his Son . . .
The second missionary was that Son, the apostle of our
*   profession . . .*
The third missionary is the Holy Ghost whom the Saviour sends
*   forth into all the earth . . .*
The fourth missionary is the church and these four missionaries
*   are all involved in one divine redemption to which we owe*
*   ourselves utterly.*

(P.T. Forsyth[1])

I THE MISSION IS GOD'S

It was the Sunday evening after Jesus' death. The disciples
of Jesus were meeting together. They had heard the bewil-
dering news from Peter and John that the tomb of Jesus was
now empty. They had listened to the incredible story of
Mary Magdalene that she had seen Jesus, spoken to him and
even touched him. But this had not been enough to break
them out of the deep fear which had set in amongst them
since Jesus' arrest. They made sure the doors were locked.
Sometime in the evening the risen Christ appeared amongst
them, spoke words of peace and then showed them the
marks of his crucifixion on his hands and side. They were
overwhelmed with joy, delight and wonder. They heard Jesus
say to them, 'As the Father sent me, so I send you.' They felt

201

him breathe upon them as he said, 'Receive the Holy Spirit' (John 20:19–22).

This resurrection story has much to tell us about the worship, mission and the trinitarian experience of God. The story has a liturgical framework. As his people meet together, Christ comes amongst them and engages with their feelings of fear and confusion by speaking peace to them. He demonstrates that he is the one who was crucified – the one who would draw all people to himself through his death (12:32). As Jesus comes to them and shows them who he is and what he has done for them they 'see him' and rejoice. They are filled with joy. They worship. But the encounter between Jesus and his followers does not just stay within the circle of their love for each other, as sweet as it is. There is an explosive propulsion built into this worshipping experience which sends them out, bursting open the doors their combined fears had firmly bolted, into the world for which God had first given his only Son (John 3:16). There is also an implosive impact upon Christ's people which empowers them to speak in Christ's name and so continue his ministry of healing the ravages of sin on the world.

Just as we are invited to step into the worship of the Trinity in which the Son glorifies the Father in the Spirit, so we are called to share in the mission of the Trinity in which the Father sends the Son by the power of the Spirit to redeem the world. The word 'mission' is derived from the Latin verb for sending. The Church is missionary because it is sent by the God who sends his Son. The Church does not have a choice about being involved in mission any more than it has a choice about being involved in worship. Worship and mission belong to the very being of the Church. We cannot be otherwise than a worshipping community and a missionary people because we have been adopted into the life of God. God's life is a life of worship overflowing into a life of mission.

202

There is no deficiency in God which causes him to create so as to have an object for his love or to find an expression for his love. The Son is the perfect object of the Father's love and the Spirit is the perfect expression of the love of the Father and the Son. But from the fullness of God's life of love he chooses to create in order to share his life of love. There is a delicate balance to be struck here. On the one hand we need to avoid implying that the creation is necessary for God, for by doing so we lose the biblical conviction that God created us by his grace not because of his need. On the other hand we need to avoid implying that the creation is inconsequential to God, as if God would be just as pleased if there were no creation. God is infinitely rich and has no poverty in need of being satisfied by the world. Yet it is in God's nature to create, for it is in the nature of love to want to give to others. Because the love between Father, Son and Holy Spirit is infinitely rich, it is also endlessly committed to enriching others.

As we saw earlier, Athanasius, and other orthodox leaders of the Church in the fourth century, grounded the divine mission – the sending of the Son and the Spirit for the creation and redemption of the world – in the eternal missions of the Son and the Spirit. The eternal movement of love by which God breathes his Word through his Spirit is extended beyond the life of God to bring new life into being. Earlier Irenaeus had described the Word and the Spirit as the two hands of God through which he first fashions the creation and then brings it to perfection by overcoming all that works for its destruction.

God creates by his powerful Word and life-giving Spirit. God chooses a people to serve him and crafts his law into their culture by communicating his Word through the inspiration of the Spirit. In the fullness of time God sends his Son to be born in the midst of the world by the agency of the Spirit, to restore the obedience of humanity and to renew the face of the earth. The sending of the Son in the power of the Spirit goes all the way to the cross. God's covenanted mission holds nothing back. The Father gives up his Son, the Son yields up his life and the Spirit bears their agony of a love disrupted by the divide of sin and death. But God will not allow his hands to be forever bound. He frees his Son from the grip of the grave and anoints him afresh with his life-giving Spirit. Through the decisive events of Jesus' death and resurrection, God's eschatological kingdom is established. God's promise of perfected life for his people is fulfilled in the risen body of Christ and the destructive forces working against his purposes are vanquished.

The story does not end here. God's mission through his Son and his Spirit continues in the life of the Church. The Church is Christ's body. We have been drawn into the life of God's kingdom; we are therefore a sign of its reality. We have been called to proclaim its reality; we are therefore a primary means by which the reality of God's kingdom is extended into the world.

At their 1988 Lambeth Conference, the bishops of the Anglican Communion gave a helpful summary of the root of the Church's mission and of its main branches:

> 'God so loved the world.' God still loves the world, and as Jesus was sent by the Father so the Church is sent by Jesus, in the name of the Father and in the power of the Holy Spirit (John 20:21). The mission of the Church is:
>
> 1. to proclaim the good news of the kingdom;
> 2. to teach, baptise and nurture new believers;
> 3. to respond to human need by loving service;
> 4. to seek to transform the unjust structures of society.[2]

Although the Lambeth list needs the addition of a fifth element along the lines of our call 'to care for the earth', it deserves credit for trying to frame an inclusive definition of mission which embraces Jesus' commands to make disciples, to love our neighbours and to confront evil. Mission involves bringing people to a conscious knowledge of and commitment to Jesus Christ within the community of the Church. Mission involves embodying and expressing the love of God, especially to those in need. Mission involves conforming human society to the values of the kingdom of God, including the proper care for the whole created order. We are called to give ourselves to this mission because this is the mission of Jesus through the power of the Spirit.

II WORSHIP AND MISSION

Worship is a primary way through which God forms us into a missionary people (a people ready to be sent) and into a missionary environment (a place where the kingdom of God is embodied and encountered). We shall focus first on how God prepares us for his work of mission through his gift of worship, and then on how God creates a place in which he can be met and his kingdom known through the experience of worship.

Worship as preparation for mission

WORSHIP RECEIVES THE MISSION OF GOD

In worship we receive the Son and the Spirit whom the Father sends for the salvation of the world. God holds us in his two hands. Christ comes into our midst as we gather in his name. He speaks his word to us. He makes himself known in the breaking of bread. He dwells in our hearts by faith. The Spirit is manifested amongst us as we worship. The Spirit enables us to confess that Christ is Lord. The Spirit reminds us of Christ's teaching. The Spirit inspires us to sing songs of worship in the name of Christ. The Spirit brings us into the presence of Christ.

At the heart of Christian worship then is the gift of communion with Christ through the work of the Spirit. In worship God ministers the healing, forgiving and ennobling presence of his Son to us through the touch of the Spirit. But to commune with Christ and to be anointed with the Spirit involves being caught up into their ministry to the world. Being recipients of the mission of God makes us also participants in the movement of his mission beyond us. As we have communion with Christ we are influenced by his way of life. As we are filled with the Spirit we are infused with his energy and enthused for his work. Christian worship is an ongoing process of commitment to Jesus and to his values. It is also an ongoing exposure to the Spirit who empowered him so that we may be equipped to live his life and to work for his values.

The mission of the Church originated from the trinitarian work of God in the worship of the Church. Luke tells us that after Jesus' ascension the disciples worshipped him. They then returned to Jerusalem where 'they were continually in the temple blessing God' (24:53). In Acts Luke gives more information about their time in Jerusalem. As well as worshipping in the temple they were 'continually devoting themselves to prayer' in an upper room (1:14). This group may have been quite large. Luke makes a point of telling us that it included some women and the brothers of Jesus. They were people who had followed Jesus, heard his teaching and seen his work. They were committed to his values. They were people who had seen him die but who had become convinced that he was alive. They loved him. As they met together on the morning of the Jewish Festival of Pentecost, the Spirit came and they experienced the presence and power of God with overwhelming intensity. There was then a movement from prayer to proclamation, from encounter with God to engagement with the world, from speaking in tongues to God to speaking to others about 'God's deeds of power' (2:11) in ways which could be understood. The Spirit who had anointed Christ was now poured out upon them so that they could both *witness to* Christ as the Messiah, the eschatological agent of God's purposes (2:32), and share in the witness of Christ to the nearness of eschatological salvation with words calling for repentance and works bringing healing (3:1–10).

Pentecost was a one-off. It established the Church as the Spirit-filled followers of Christ. As the foundational moment in the Church's history it cannot be repeated but as the defining dynamic of the Church it has to be appropriated in the contemporary life of God's people. We do so by meeting in Christ's name and allowing the Holy Spirit to empower us to engage in the mission for which God sent his Son.

WORSHIP CELEBRATES THE MISSION OF GOD

The gospel of God's great goodness in creating and redeeming the world is not a piece of information needing to be catalogued. Neither is it a piece of knowledge requiring dispassionate discussion. It is a truth demanding celebration.

Whenever we hear really good news our natural instinct is to want to celebrate. By celebrating we *acknowledge* that the news is important. It has made a difference to people's lives and so deserves to be marked out as significant and valuable. By celebrating we are helped to *own* the good thing that has happened. It is not just a theoretical idea. It is an actual reality which in some way or another will affect us. It requires acceptance and possession. By celebrating we *enjoy* whatever has happened. It has created a new state of affairs with a whole new vista of opportunities. As we celebrate we both express our delight in this new world of possibilities and begin to step into them and start living in the light of them.

207

The collapse of the oppressive political systems in Eastern Europe was marked by remarkable scenes of celebration as people filled the streets of one city after another to acknowledge, own and enjoy the end of an old order which had steadily constrained their humanity and the beginning of a new one which held out great hopes for freedom and prosperity. How much more with the good news of Christ with its significance for the whole of creation and its promise which will not fade or disappoint? By celebrating the gospel in worship we acknowledge that it is true. We affirm that it is not just a heartening story but a set of events forged in history. As we worship we own these events and claim them as our story. Through worship we enjoy the new way of living which the gospel brings.

These are all essential elements enabling us to fulfil our role in God's mission. We affirm the breadth and depth of God's goodness to the world. We accept that we are beneficiaries of God's goodness. We allow ourselves to enter into the purposes for good which God has for us in Christ. In this way God's mission becomes the object of our praise. As Martin Luther said, 'faith cannot be silent'.[3] We sing of our salvation. Each act of worship becomes a signal witnessing to the world that God's kingdom has come in Christ. God's mission also becomes the object of our prayer. We pray for the complete manifestation of the kingdom of God and we commit ourselves to play our part in its coming.

WORSHIP RESTRUCTURES US FOR MISSION
It is difficult not to be affected by the people with whom we spend time. There is only so much time we can spend with people who are seriously depressed before we feel ourselves being brought low. Similarly, there is something infectious about people's joy and laughter. We are lifted by them. Every responsible parent works hard to avoid unwholesome influences on their children because we know that human

nature is like a sponge. We absorb what is around us. We are changed by the company we keep and the environment in which we are placed.

It is the same with worship. Spending time with God and his people changes us. A process of osmosis sets in as we gradually absorb the ways of God and find his image being restored in us. His image, of course, is trinitarian. His life is a relational life, a life of giving and receiving love. As we encounter God in worship we discover something of the relational life in which God eternally exists. We also experience the way God is relational towards us. God does not stand aloof from our worship, disinterested in our praise and unaffected by our prayers. God has gone to the most costly lengths imaginable to establish our liturgical relationship with him. He has made our hearts restless till they find their rest in him, as Augustine said. Neither has he allowed himself to rest until his people enter into the joy of his worship.

When we begin to glimpse something of the yearning with which God longs for us to live in loving relation to him, we begin to break out of the self-preoccupation which so easily imprisons us in a lonely cell of personal protection. In one sense sin has made us all introverts – individuals centred on our own needs and concerns. Engagement with God in worship turns us into extroverts in the sense that we become people who are orientated outwards. We learn what it means to give and to receive. We are prepared to go out of ourselves in the praise of God and to open ourselves to the blessing of God. This restructuring of our lives in genuinely relational ways through worship is simultaneously tested out in the company of the Church. 'Those who say "I love God", and hate their brothers and sisters, are liars' (1 John 4:20). Our engagement with God in worship, even when alone, is always part of an interconnected whole. If the quality of our relationships with other members of the worshipping body of Christ is not affected for good by our worship of God, then our worship has been only skin deep and God has been kept at a distance. When we allow ourselves to embrace God and to be embraced by God, the coldness of our hearts towards others begins to thaw.

The success of the restructuring of our lives outwards is also challenged as soon as the worship ends. If we have had dealings with the God who has covenanted himself towards his created work, then we will know that his love does not end with us or even with the whole of his Church but extends throughout the earth. The extent to which we are willing to commit ourselves to God's covenant with all that he has made and to his will 'to gather up all things in Christ, things in heaven and on earth' (Eph. 1:10), will be a measure of the depth of our involvement with God in worship.

WORSHIP INSPIRES US FOR MISSION

Because worship is the enjoyment of the gospel, it is a boundless source of inspiration for the mission of communicating the gospel to the world and establishing the gospel in the world. The heart of the gospel is Paul's simple summary that God is 'for us' (e.g. Rom. 8:32). The dynamic of worship expands the horizons not just of what this means for us but of what it means for God.

We said earlier that the Father chooses to extend the love he has for the Son and the Spirit, and which they have for each other, into the creative act of bringing other life into being. God, therefore, has directed himself towards his creation and committed himself to its good. The creation is designed to be in relationship with God and to reflect the just and liberating pattern of God's relationships in its life. Human rejection of God's gift of relationship causes a profound disruption not only in the relation between humanity and God but in the whole order of relationships in the world. Nevertheless, God's will for the well-being of the world is such that he works, at great cost, for the restoration of the relationships he intended for the world. As we participate in the gift of worship through Christ and in the Spirit, we enter the reordered pattern which God wills for us. We relate to him. We relate to other people. We relate to the rest of his creation.

During the Apartheid years of South Africa a wrongly ordered set of relationships was institutionalized by political ideology and the law of the land. When black, white and coloured Christians worshipped together as one community they were demonstrating that people can be freed from even the fiercest structures which disrupt human relationships. They experienced the same reality as Paul had witnessed in the common worship of Jew and Gentile. Christ, he explained, had broken down the walls of hostility which divide the peoples and formed them into one new humanity with equal access to the Father in the one Spirit (Eph. 2:14–18). The reconciled relationships which South African Christians experienced in their worshipping communities was both a sign that a different order of relationships was possible and an impetus for people to work for the day when the life of the Church would become the practice of the country.

Because God has committed himself to our well-being he has opened himself to us and allowed himself to be affected by us. His heart is moved by the pain caused through our wrongly ordered relationships. In Christ he suffers the consequences of our rejection of his pattern for relationships and submits to a legalized murder by which he experiences the alienating character of death in its crudest form. And God's heart is also moved by the joy which comes from rightly ordered relationships. Worship is the sign that these are coming into being because, as we have said, in worship we are acknowledging the purpose of God's creative and redemptive work for the world and taking hold of the relationship of love which he has restored with us. Our worship brings delight to God. As we live out our baptism into the worshipping life of his Son through the gift of his Spirit, God is well pleased with us. We bring him joy.

The joy we bring to God in our praise is like the gift a child gives, say of a painting, to her parents. Their child is in a sense created by them. All the materials she has used have been provided by them. Mother and Father may have spent time with the child encouraging her to paint and giving her ideas about what she might paint, even showing her how to paint, yet still the picture brings joy. Still the picture is a new contribution to the family's life. The gift of our praise is also a new contribution to the life of God. Of course it would not have happened if God had not enabled it and yet it is still a free act of the creation bringing a new dimension to God's glory that would not have been there without us. Our worship is truly for the increase of God's glory.

This does not mean that God is deficient without our praise and therefore dependent upon it – to think in such ways is to constrain God within finite categories which assume God's glory has a limit which is already necessarily reached in the perfection of his life. But God's glory and God's perfection are not limited in this way. They are boundless and expansive – infinite, in other words. The glory which the Father, Son and Spirit give to each other is not a static repetition of mutual honour. It is a movement of praise which multiplies God's infinity. It is this divine dynamic 'upwards' which gives God the capacity to participate in the movement 'downwards' in creation and redemption. Because Father, Son and Holy Spirit eternally increase their glory through their everlasting enjoyment and adoration of each other, God is, as it were, structured to receive glory from his creation. Through his work of creation and redemption God gathers a glory to himself which collides with the ever expanding glory which Father, Son and Holy Spirit ascribe to each other in their eternal song of praise.[4]

When we see pictures of the immensity of the universe it is difficult not to be overwhelmed. We cannot imagine how it can be so vast and yet include a place where we can have value and significance. It is even more so when we consider God. It is like looking through Hubble's telescope with one eye and through a powerful microscope with the other. We see such limitless immensity in God which is beyond our wildest imaginings and yet, as we look at God's dealings with the world, we see something of what John Donne saw when he wrote of Mary, pregnant with Jesus, 'immensity cloysterd in thy deare wombe'.[5] God covenants himself to his creation to produce a people of praise. He directs his riches to our enrichment. He creates by the two hands of his Word and Spirit and he comes amongst us in his Word and his Spirit to recreate us. He indwells us by his Word and his Spirit. He binds himself to us in love. He gives himself 'for us'.

In worship God's immensity is extended to us in a touch of intimacy. We are drawn into a real relationship of mutuality with him where we not only receive from God but also genuinely give to God that which he cannot have without us. Such news of God's goodness to us cannot be kept to ourselves. It must be shared.

Worship as an environment for mission

Worship is not the same as mission. Worship addresses God. Mission addresses the world. Nevertheless, although not identical, worship and mission are closely connected. The way in which worship prepares the Church to be a missionary people is clearly one aspect of their relationship but there are at least three other ways in which they feed into each other.

213

First, the worshipping community embodies the kingdom of God. When people are sharing in authentic Christian worship they express the reordered way of living which Christ was sent to bring by his ministry in the Spirit. The mission of God becomes visible and tangible in a community of people reconciled to God, to each other and to the rest of creation. The Church's worship should be a living witness to the content of the Church's message – an environment in which God's way of doing things can be seen and heard. More than this, God himself can be encountered in the worship of the Church because the Church is the temple in which God dwells. Temples are built for worship. As the people of God worship, God inhabits their praise (Ps. 22:3), reveals his glory (2 Chron. 7:1–3), speaks his word (1 Cor. 14:25) and is made known in the love they share for each other (1 John 4:12). Worship therefore provides an opportunity not only to see the life of the kingdom in action but to meet the King of the kingdom in person.

Secondly, worship and mission are part of one tidal movement involving a going out and a coming in. Worship sends us out into the world to live and speak the good news of the kingdom. Mission draws the world into the life of the Church so that it can hear more of Christ, be touched further by his Spirit and enter into the praise of his Father. The whole process by which people come to Christ and begin to live in his way interacts at several points with the worship of the Church. It has to do so for two reasons. The first is because the ministries of the worshipping life of the Church are ways in which Christ is made known, they are places where Christ can be met. The second is because following Christ means being part of his body. Christian initiation involves membership of the Church. Whether these various intersections are ritualized in the catechumenate programmes used by some of the churches or take place through the natural course of continuing contact

214

with and increasing commitment to the life of the Church, worship will play an integral part in the making of new disciples.

Thirdly, worship provides an environment in which the Church can give thanks for the advance of God's mission in the world. This may be when new believers respond to God with praise and joy for the salvation they have received, just as the man crippled from birth burst into praise when he was healed through the ministry of Peter and John (Acts 3:8). Or it may be when a whole congregation gives thanks for the signs of God's kingdom breaking into the conditions of the world, bringing light into darkness and peace into violence, just as the first Christians gave thanks for the release of Peter and John from prison after they had been arrested for speaking and acting in the name of Christ (Acts 3:23–31).

Worship itself is a sign of eschatological salvation. It is a sign that people have entered God's kingdom of rightly ordered relationships. It is a sign that God is amongst his people living and active in their midst, present in their love and inviting them deeper into his life. It is a sign that God's kingdom is being established on earth because people are giving thanks for its presence in their lives and in the lives of others. However, like every sign of salvation it is stamped with the imprint of a kingdom which has truly come and yet which is still to come fully. All the evidence our worship brings of the nearness of the kingdom is also matched by examples of its distance. The worship of the Church is not yet the worship of heaven. Even the most inspiring and uplifting acts of worship are fraught with imperfections and inadequacies. None the less, the failings of our worship do not deny the claim that as we worship God we participate in the salvation of God's kingdom, they simply reinforce our prayer for the kingdom to come fully.

Worship is a sign of our future salvation both in the sense

of signalling its presence and in the sense of showing its character. Because worship is focused attention on the God who saves, it is a concentrated example of what it means to be saved. Salvation involves being redeemed into the rightly ordered pattern of relationships which God intends for the world. In worship we can see these relationships coming into being as the image of the one we are worshipping is restored in us and we begin to mirror his life of love.

God wants us to be properly related to him. This involves more than believing that God exists and more than accepting that God is the guarantee of the moral order of the universe. It involves us giving ourselves over to him and receiving all that he longs to give us. This is the essence of worship. It is made possible through the ministry of Christ and the Spirit. Our giving and receiving are perfected through Christ's giving and receiving from the Father and they are connected with Christ's giving and receiving through the work of the Spirit who brings us into fellowship with Christ and with all his work.

God wants us to be properly related to each other. This involves more than acknowledging the dignity of our fellow human beings; more even than avoiding conflict and working for justice. It involves sharing in a common life of commitment to mutual well-being. This is the nature of worship. We give to God and receive from him as members of the body of Christ in the fellowship of the Holy Spirit. Christ's body is a community of care in which his healing and reconciling ministry overcomes the fragmentation of the world and binds each to the other in the freedom of love. The fellowship of the Spirit is a communion of people of different sexes, ages, social positions and races (Acts 2:17–18, Gal. 3:28) who have been baptized into a new social order where all belong equally to God.

God wants us to be properly related to the whole created order. This involves more than affirming the value of creation and working for its preservation. It means honouring and hallowing the creation so that its true identity as the work of God's hands can be acknowledged and its true role of displaying God's glory and singing his praise can be found. This is what happens in worship. The gifts of God in creation are 'received with thanksgiving' and 'sanctified by God's word and by prayer' (1 Tim. 4:4–5). We bring creation before God to celebrate it as the work of his hands and to anticipate the day when God will renew all that he has made. The song we will sing then will be the same song we sing now – the song of adoration to the 'three person'd God' which unites the children of the earth with the angels of heaven:

Holy, holy, holy Lord
God of power and might,
heaven and earth are full of your glory.
Hosanna in the highest.[6]

217

Notes
ᴏᴏᴏᴏᴏᴏᴏᴏᴏ

CHAPTER 1: The Trinity and Worship

1. On Prayer, 61, cited in Olivier Clément, *The Roots of Christian Mysticism* (London: New City, 1993), p. 184.
2. Michael Ignatieff, '20/20': 'Talking about the Century', BBC Radio 4, 15 January 1997.
3. 'The Little Flowers' in *The Writings and Early Biographies on St Francis*, edited by Marion Habig (London: SPCK, 1979), p. 1446.
4. Michael Ignatieff, '20/20'.
5. See Grace Davie, *Religion in Britain since 1945: Believing without Belonging* (Oxford: Blackwell, 1994).
6. Further evidence of the renaissance in trinitarian theology will appear in the notes of this book and in a selection of the more accessible writing on the Trinity, particularly that which relates to worship, recommended at the end of the book. A useful summary of some recent trinitarian theology can be found in John Thompson, *Modern Trinitarian Perspectives* (Oxford: OUP, 1994).
7. Walter Kasper, *The God of Jesus Christ* (London: SCM, 1984), p. 233.
8. Thomas F. Torrance, *The Christian Doctrine of God: One Being in Three Persons* (Edinburgh: T&T Clark, 1996), p. 31.
9. Robert W. Jenson, *The Triune Identity: God According to the Gospel* (Philadelphia: Fortress Press, 1982), p. xii.
10. *God of Jesus Christ*, pp. 281, 305.
11. *Christian Doctrine of God*, p. 19.
12. A strong statement of the connection between worship and trinitarian theology can be found in C.M. La Cugna and K. McDonnell, 'Returning from the "Far Country": Theses for a Contemporary Trinitarian Theology', *Scottish Journal of Theology*, 41 (1988), 191–215 and Catherine Mowry La Cugna, *God For Us: The Trinity and Christian*

Life (San Francisco: Harper, 1991). For a very helpful analysis of the role of worship in the theological task as a whole, see Daniel W. Hardy, 'The Foundation of Cognition and Ethics in Worship' in his *God's Ways with the World: Thinking and Practising Christian Faith* (Edinburgh: T&T Clark, 1996), pp. 5–30.

13. *On Prayer,* 61.

14. *Saint Augustine: The Trinity,* translated by Stephen McKenna (Washington: Catholic University of America Press, 1963).

15. Karl Barth, *Church Dogmatics* I.1 (Edinburgh: T&T Clark, 1975), p. 450.

16. From 'Holy Sonnets (Divine Meditations)' by John Donne, in *The Complete English Poems of John Donne,* edited by C.A. Patrides (London: J.M. Dent, 1985), p. 443.

17. For a clear presentation of this view, see Sallie McFague, *Models of God: Theology for an Ecological, Nuclear Age* (London: SCM, 1985). For a persuasive reply see Colin Gunton, 'Proteus and Procrustes: A Study in the Dialectic of Language in Disagreement with Sallie McFague' in *Speaking the Christian God,* edited by Alvin F. Kimel, Jr (Grand Rapids: Eerdmans, 1992), pp. 65–80.

18. See Janet Martin Soskice, 'Can a Feminist Call God "Father"?', in *Speaking the Christian God,* edited by Kimel, pp. 81–94 (p. 88).

19. Paul Ricoeur, 'Fatherhood: From Phantasm to Symbol', in *The Conflict of Interpretation: Essays in Hermeneutics,* edited by D. Ihde (Evanston: Northwestern University Press, 1974), pp. 490–1, cited by Soskice, 'Can a Feminist Call God "Father"?', p. 90.

20. 'The Trinity and Mystic Pietà' (1512). The painting can be found in the National Gallery, London.

CHAPTER 2: The Shape of Worship in the New Testament

1. See Acts 18:1–11, 1 and 2 Corinthians.

2. This is a point strongly made in James D.G. Dunn, *Christology in the Making,* second edition (London: SCM, 1980).

3. Warning signs such as these are clearly given in Paul Bradshaw, *The Search for the Origins of Christian Worship* (London: SPCK, 1992), pp. 30–55.

4. *Commentaries on the Epistle of Paul the Apostle to the Romans by John*

Calvin, translated and edited by John Owen (Edinburgh: Calvin Translation Society, 1849), pp. 299–300.

5. See Alasdair Heron, 'The Biblical Basis for the Doctrine of the Trinity', in *The Forgotten Trinity: A Selection of Papers*, edited by Alasdair I.C. Heron (London: BCC/CCBI, 1991), pp. 33–43.

6. Robert W. Jenson, *The Triune Identity: God According to the Gospel* (Philadelphia: Fortress Press, 1982), p. 10.

7. E.g. Joseph A. Fitzmyer, *Romans: A New Translation and Commentary*, The Anchor Bible (London: Geoffrey Chapman, 1993); James D.G. Dunn, *Romans 8:1–8*, Word Biblical Commentary Vol. 38 (Dallas: Word Books, 1988); Ernst Kasemann, *Commentary on Romans* (London: SCM, 1980).

8. *The Epistle to the Romans*, translated by Edwin C. Hoskyns (London: OUP, 1933), p. 299.

9. *Lectures on Romans: Luther's Works Vol. 25*, General Editors, Jaroslav Pelikan and Helmut Lehmann (Missouri: Concordia Publishing House, 1972), p. 358.

10. *Commentaries*, p. 298.

11. Joachim Jeremias, *The Prayers of Jesus* (London: SCM, 1967), pp. 11–65.

12. *Christology*, p. 32.

13. E.g. Dunn, *Romans*; Fitzmyer, *Romans*; C.K. Barrett, *The Epistle to the Romans*, Black's New Testament Commentaries (London: A&C Black, 1987). Fee argues the case for a reference to glossalalia but admits that the case is not fully proven; see Gordon G. Fee, *God's Empowering Presence: The Holy Spirit in the Letters of Paul* (Peabody, Mass.: Hendrickson, 1994), pp. 572–86.

14. *Triune Identity*, p. 51.

15. Fee, *God's Empowering Presence*, p. 586.

16. *The Sunday Missal* (London: Collins, 1975).

17. Martin Hengel, *Between Jesus and Paul* (London: SCM, 1982), p. 91.

18. *Jesus and Paul*, p. 92.

19. E.g. 4:23–31; 5:29–32; 6:3–6; 7:56–9; 8:14–17; 10:44–5; 11:11–26; 13:1–3; 15:1–29; 16:1–10; 19:1–7; 20:17–24; 21:7–14; 28:23–8.

20. The question of whether Paul was the author of all the letters attributed to him in the New Testament has been, of course, an area of scholarly debate for over two hundred years. The point at which this becomes a significant issue for my argument is over the matter of dating. In this chapter I am focusing on early material in order

to uncover something of the nature of Christian worship in its earlier years, e.g. from the death of Christ (*c.* 33 CE to *c.* 65 CE). Hence I have chosen not to draw on the Pastoral Epistles (1 and 2 Timothy) because many argue that they reflect the Church's life and are therefore unlikely for this and for other reasons to have been written by Paul. The case against Pauline authorship is by no means conclusive but in order to use only secure evidence I will avoid them in this chapter. However, I do include Ephesians and Colossians in my material, partly because their Pauline authorship is less problematic than the Pastorals and partly because they reflect a pattern of worship consistent with other evidence from earlier material. For further discussion of Ephesians and Colossians see note 26.

21. Richard J. Bauckham, *Jude, 2 Peter,* Word Biblical Commentaries (Milton Keynes: Word Publishing, 1986), pp. 3–17.

22. For a discussion of the phrase 'in the Spirit' in early Christian literature see Richard Bauckham, *The Climax of Prophecy: Studies in the Book of Revelation* (Edinburgh: T&T Clark, 1993), pp. 150–9.

23. Geoffrey Wainwright, *Doxology: A Systematic Theology* (London: Epworth Press, 1980), p. 91.

24. 'God's empowering presence' is the title of the book. For Fee's rationale see pp. 5–9.

25. See Hengel, *Jesus and Paul,* pp. 79–81. See also Fee, *Empowering Presence,* pp. 648–57.

26. See Hengel, *Jesus and Paul,* p. 81; Fee, *Empowering Presence,* p. 722. We need to note that whereas Ephesians refers to songs being sung 'to the Lord' (probably meaning Christ), Colossians, in a very similar passage, refers to them being sung only to God (3:16). At this point the question of the disputed Pauline authorship of Ephesians becomes a potential problem for my argument. For example, if (a) Ephesians was not written by Paul himself but was actually written by someone standing within, as it were, his school of theology and attributed to him as its theological source or authority at a later stage in the century (say 80–90 CE), and (b) Colossians is genuinely Pauline and therefore can be dated in the middle of the century, the change from 'to God' (in Colossians) to 'to the Lord' (in Ephesians) may indicate a development towards a more Christ-centred worship as the century proceeded. However, as there is no scholarly concensus over the authorship of Ephesians

– or, for that matter, Colossians – I do not feel under any reasonable pressure to exclude Ephesians from my package of early evidence about the early life of the Church. On this whole question of authorship and date, it is worth saying that the probability that Ephesians refers to the worship of Christ is not a strong argument for it not to have been written by Paul (and therefore to be of a later date) because there is sufficient evidence of Christ-centred worship in undisputed Pauline writings and in other material to establish its existence in the early years of Christian worship.

27. Joachim Jeremias, *The Eucharistic Words of Jesus* (London: SCM, 1966), p. 253. See also C.K. Barrett, *A Commentary on the First Epistle to the Corinthians* (London: A&C Black, 1971), second edition, pp. 270–1.

28. *Romans*, p. 18.

29. In the rest of Acts the Christological and the pneumatological are held together. The relationship is not always tidy. The Spirit falls on Cornelius's household before the people are baptized. The Samaritans and the Ephesians undergo a baptism before the Spirit comes to them. But the clear impression is that the early Christian communities' experience of baptism was one in which people were brought into a new relationship with God through the continuing significance of Christ and by the action of the Spirit.

Paul's references to baptism are quite similar to Luke's in Acts. Baptism is both 'into Christ' (Rom. 6:3; Gal. 3:27) and 'in the one Spirit' (1 Cor.12:3). It involves the believer in the death of the old humanity and the raising to life of the new humanity which 'lives to God' (Rom. 6:10).

CHAPTER 3: The Pattern, Precedents and Perspectives of Worship in the New Testament

1. Richard Bauckham, 'The Worship of Jesus' in *The Anchor Bible Dictionary*, Vol. 3, edited by David Noel Freedman, pp. 812–9; R.T. France, 'The Worship of Jesus: A Neglected Factor in Christological Debate?' in *Christ the Lord: Studies in Christology*, edited by H.H. Rowden (Leicester: IVP, 1982), pp. 17–36; Hengel, *Jesus and Paul*; Larry W. Hurtado, *One God, One Lord: Early Christian Devotion and Ancient Jewish Monotheism* (London: SCM, 1988); Ralph Martin, *Worship in the Early Church*, revised edition (Grand Rapids: Eerd-

mans, 1983); N.T. Wright, *The New Testament and the People of God* (London: SPCK, 1992), pp. 359–70, 444–76.

2. Useful studies of hymnody in early Christian worship can be found in James H. Charlesworth, 'A Prolegomenon to a New Study of the Jewish Background of the Hymns and Prayers in the New Testament', *JJS* 33 (1982), 265–85; Hengel, *Jesus and Paul*, pp. 78–96; Ralph Martin, 'Some Reflections on New Testament Hymns' in *Christ the Lord*, edited by Rowden, pp. 37–49.

3. E.g. Rom. 8:34b; Eph.1:20–2; Col.1:15–20; 1 Tim. 3:16; Heb.1:5–13, 2:6–8; 1 Pet. 3:18–22; Rev. 4:8,11, 5:9–10,12,13, 7:12.

4. This view, popularized by Rudolf Bultmann (see his *Theology of the New Testament*, Vol.1 (London: SCM, 1952), pp. 166ff.) was held by many in the History of Religion School (i.e. the comparative approach to religious concepts popular in the nineteenth century and for much of the twentieth which assumed that clear lines of development could be determined between the religious ideas of different traditions).

5. In addition to the studies referred to in note 1 see: Richard Bauckham, *The Theology of the Book of Revelation* (Cambridge: CUP, 1993), 'The Worship of Jesus in Apocalyptic Christianity', *NTS* 27 (1981), pp. 322–41.

6. See James D.G. Dunn, *Christology in the Making*, second edition (London: SCM, 1989), pp. 258–61. See also Alan F. Segal, *Two Powers in Heaven* (Leiden: E.J. Brill, 1977), pp. 147–55.

7. Isidore Epstein, *Judaism: A Historical Presentation* (Harmondsworth: Penguin Books, 1959), p. 134.

8. *New Testament and the People of God*, p. 248.

9. *New Testament and the People of God*, p. 259. See also Bauckham, 'Worship of Jesus in Apocalyptic Christianity', pp. 322–3.

10. Useful studies can be found in J.F. Balchin, 'Paul, Wisdom and Christ', in *Christ the Lord*, edited by Rowden, pp. 204–19; Dunn, *Christology*, 163–250; Hurtado, *One God, One Lord*, pp. 41–50.

11. Useful studies can be found in Dunn, *Christology*, pp. 98–162; Hurtado, *One God, One Lord*, pp. 51–92; Dan Cohn-Sherbok and Lavina Cohn-Sherbok, *Jewish and Christian Mysticism: An Introduction* (New York: Continuum, 1994), pp. 17–33.

12. See Richard Bauckham's 1996 Didsbury Lectures, *God Crucified: Monotheism and Christology in the New Testament* to be published by Paternoster Press/Eerdmans, 1998.

13. Useful studies can be found in R.E. Clements, *God and Temple* (Oxford: Basil Blackwell, 1965); Cohn-Sherbok, *Jewish and Christian Mysticism*; Jon D. Levenson, 'The Jerusalem Temple in Devotional and Visionary Experience' in *Jewish Spirituality*, edited by Arthur Green (London: Routledge and Kegan Paul, 1986), pp. 32–61; E.P. Sanders, *Jesus and Judaism* (London: SCM, 1985); Samuel Terrien, *The Elusive Presence* (San Francisco: Harper and Row, 1978); Wright, *New Testament and the People of God*, pp. 224–43.

14. 'Jerusalem Temple', p. 47.

15. The claim that first-century Judaism believed itself to be still awaiting the real return from Israel is argued forcibly and convincingly in Wright, *New Testament and the People of God*.

16. *One God, One Lord*, p. 100.

17. For a fuller treatment of Hebrew's liturgical theology see my 'The Cross, Our Worship and Our Living', in *The Atonement in the Modern World*, edited by John Goldingay (London: SPCK, 1995), pp. 111–27.

18. See e.g. Royce Gordon Gruenler, *The Trinity in the Gospel of John* (Grand Rapids: Baker Book House, 1986).

19. B.F. Westcott, *The Gospel of John* (London: John Murray, 1890), p. 206.

20. *Gospel of John*, p. 200.

21. From 'Rite A' in *The Alternative Service Book 1980*.

22. See the clear and detailed analysis of Revelation in the work of Richard Bauckham (upon which I draw): 'Worship of Jesus in Apocalytic Christianity': *Climax of Prophecy; Theology of Revelation*.

23. See e.g. John Sweet, *Revelation* (London: SCM, 1979), pp. 41–2.

24. *Theology of Revelation*, p. 60.

CHAPTER 4: The Worship of the Evolving Church

1. First Apology, 67 in *Early Christian Fathers*, Library of Christian Classics Vol. I, edited by Cyril. E. Richardson (London: SCM, 1955).

2. Quoted by Richard Bauckham in 'Worship of Jesus', p. 816.

3. *Anonymous Sermon: Known As II Clement*, 1:1 in *Early Fathers*, Library of Christian Classics Vol. I, edited by Cyril. E. Richardson (London: SCM, 1955), p. 193. For the sake of clarity I have modernized the English in some of the older translations of the Fathers which follow.

Notes

4. *I Clement* 46:5 in *Early Fathers*, p. 65.

5. *Ephesians* 4:2 in *Early Fathers*, p. 89.

6. *Ephesians* 8:9 in *Early Fathers*, p. 90.

7. *Ephesians* 18:2 in *Early Fathers*, p. 92.

8. *Didache* 7:1 in *Early Fathers*, p. 174.

9. The *Didache's* teaching on the Eucharist can be found in Chs. 9, 10 and 14.

10. *The Martyrdom of Polycarp*, 8:2 in *Early Fathers*, p. 152.

11. *Martyrdom of Polycarp*, 9–12 in *Early Fathers*, pp. 152–4.

12. *Martyrdom of Polycarp*, 14 in *Early Fathers*, p. 154.

13. *The Apostolic Tradition of Hippolytus*, 4:35, edited by Burton Scott Easton (Cambridge: CUP, 1934).

14. *The Didascalia* 1.32 in *The Liturgical Portions of the Didascalia*, edited by Sebastian Brock and Michael Vasey (Bramcote: Grove Books, 1982).

15. *The First Apology of Justin the Martyr*, 61, in *Early Fathers*, pp. 282–3.

16. *The Demonstration of the Apostolic Preaching*, 6. This translation is from Alister E. McGrath, *The Christian Theology Reader* (Oxford: Blackwells, 1995), p. 95. For an example of the trinitarian confession in the rite of baptism see *Apostolic Tradition*, 3:21.

17. 1.10:1–2; see also 1.22:1, 3. Preface – 3.1:1.

18. 3.4:1; see also 1.22:1, 3.5:1, 3.15:1.

19. 4.6:7.

20. *The Demonstration of the Apostolic Preaching*, 7, edited by J. Armitage Robinson (London: SPCK, 1920).

21. *Demonstration*, 5; see also *Against Heresies*, 5.18:2.

22. *Against Praxaeus*, 26, edited by Ernest Evans (London: SPCK, 1943).

23. *Against Praxaeus*, 11, 13.

24. *Demonstration*, 97.

25. *Against Heresies*, 2.32:4.

26. *Against Heresies*, 2.32:5.

27. *Apostolic Tradition*, 1:3.

28. E.g. *On Prayer*, 2–3, in Ante-Nicene Christian Library, Vol. XI, edited by Alexander Roberts and James Donaldson (Edinburgh: T&T Clark, 1869), pp. 178–204.

29. *On Prayer*, 15.4 in *Alexandrian Christianity*, Library of Christian Classics Vol. II, edited by John E.L. Oulton and Henry Chadwick (London: SCM, 1954), pp. 270–1.

30. *Dialogue with Heraclides*, 130 in *Alexandrian Christianity*, p. 440.

31. In fact mid-Platonism saw the whole of reality as emanating from the pure being of God with all things possessing, in lesser degrees, a dimension of divinity. This was reflected in Origen's thought and is most clearly detected in his teaching that all rational creatures, including the devil, eventually will be saved and restored to their true source in God from which they (necessarily) derive immortal being.

32. *Addai and Mari – The Anaphora of the Apostles*, edited by Bryan D. Spinks (Bramcote: Grove Books, 1980).

33. *First Apology*, 67 in *Early Fathers*, p. 287.

34. *Apostolic Tradition*, 1:4. This translation is from *Prayers of the Eucharist*, edited by R.C.D. Jasper and C.J. Cuming (New York: OUP, 1980), 2nd edition, pp. 22–3.

35. See also *Addai and Mari*.

36. E.g. *Didache*, 14, in *Early Fathers*, p. 178.

37. See *Against Heresies*, 4.17–4:18.

38. Richard Hanson, 'The Achievement of Orthodoxy in the Fourth Century' in *The Making of Orthodoxy*, edited by Rowan Williams (Cambridge: CUP, 1989), pp. 142–156. See also his *The Search for the Christian Doctrine of God* (Edinburgh: T&T Clark, 1988).

39. From Arius' *Thalia*, quoted by Athanasius in *Against the Arians* 1:5–6. Athanasius' writings quoted can be found in *The Nicene and Post-Nicene Fathers*, Vol. IV, Second Series, edited by Philip Schaff and Henry Wace (Grand Rapids: Eerdmans, 1881) and C.R.B. Shapland, *The Letters to Serapion Concerning the Holy Spirit* (London: Epworth Press, 1951).

40. The full text of the creed, together with the accompanying anathemas, can be found in Henry Bettensen, *Documents of the Christian Church*, 2nd edition (Oxford: OUP, 1963), p. 25.

41. For an important recent study of Athanasius' thought see Alvyn Pettersen, *Athanasius* (London: Geoffrey Chapman, 1995).

42. T.F. Torrance, *The Trinitarian Faith* (Edinburgh: T&T Clark, 1993), p. 29.

43. *To Serapion* 1:20.

44. *To Serapion* 1:20.

45. *Defence of Nicea* 2. See also *Against the Arians* 1.17, 3.6.

46. *Against the Arians* 2.34.

47. Peter Widdicombe, *The Fatherhood of God from Origen to Athanasius* (Oxford: Clarenden Press, 1994), p. 159.

48. *Against the Arians* 2.1–2, 41–3, 3.6. See also Pettersen, *Athanasius*, pp. 166–178, 192–4.
49. E.g. *Against the Arians* 2.41; *To Serapion* 1.26–7.
50. *To Serapion* 1.23–1.30. See also Rowan Williams, 'Baptism in the Arian Controversy' in *Arianism After Arius,* edited by Michel Barnes and Daniel Williams (Edinburgh: T&T Clark, 1993), pp. 149–80.
51. Sources for the liturgies mentioned in this section are: Jasper and Cuming, *Prayers of the Eucharist* for the *Egyptian Fragments* (earliest examples of *The Liturgy of St Mark* and *The Liturgy of St James*); Burton Scott Easton, *The Apostolic Tradition*; Anton Hänggi and IrmGard Pahl, *Prex Eucharistica* (Éditions Universitaires Fribourg Suisse, 1968) for the *Anaphora of Basil*; and the following Alcuin/GROW Liturgical Studies (Bramcote: Grove Books) – R.J.S. Barrett-Leonard, *The Sacramentary of Serapion* (1993), W. Jardine Grisbrooke, *The Liturgical Portions of the Apostolic Constitutions* (1990), *The Canons of Hippolytus,* edited by Paul Bradshaw (1987), Grant Sperry-White, *The Testamentum Domini* (1991).
52. *On the Spirit* 7.3, 7.16. The works of Cappadocians quoted can be found in *Nicene and Post-Nicene Fathers* Vols. V, VII and VIII.
53. *Letter* 258.2.
54. *On the Spirit* 10.26.
55. *On the Spirit* 10.24.
56. *On the Spirit* 27.68.
57. *On the Spirit* 26.63.
58. *Fifth Theological Oration* 14.
59. *Fifth Theological Oration* 3.
60. *Fifth Theological Oration* 28.
61. On *'Not Three Gods'.*
62. Letter 38.3, sometimes ascribed to Gregory of Nyssa.
63. See particularly, Gregory of Nazianzus, *Fifth Theological Oration* 9.
64. John D. Zizioulas, *Being as Communion* (London: DLT, 1985).
65. Colin E. Gunton, *The Promise of Trinitarian Theology* (Edinburgh: T&T Clark, 1991), p. 10.
66. The E.L.L.C. (English Language Liturgical Consultation) 1988 translation.
67. *Against the Arians* 1.18.

Notes

CHAPTER 5: The Glory of God

1. Mercury Records Ltd (London).
2. Collect of 17th Sunday after Trinity, *The Christian Year: Calendar, Collects and Lectionary* (London: CHP, 1997).
3. See *Saint Augustine: Confessions*, translated by Henry Chadwick (Oxford: OUP, 1991), I.i (1).
4. *The Trinity*, 4.7.11.
5. *The Trinity*, 14.2.4. On the theme of seeking and seeing God's face see 1.12.31, 9.1.1, 14.14.20–4, 15.2.2; 1.8.16, 1.12.28, 8.4.6, 15.11.20, 15.23.44.
6. David Silk, *Prayers for Use at the Alternative Services* (London: Mowbray, 1986), no. 106.
7. This translation (and emphasis) is Walter Brueggemann's from his *Genesis: Interpretation* (Atlanta: John Knox Press, 1982).
8. For a comparison and (an unduly) strong contrast between the two, see Samuel Terrien, *Elusive Presence*
9. *Theological Dictionary of the New Testament*, edited by Gerhard Kittel (Grand Rapids, Michigan: Eerdmans, 1966), Vol. II, p. 248.
10. David M. Hay, *Glory at the Right Hand* (New York: Abingdon Press, 1973), p. 155.
11. Arthur Michael Ramsey, *The Glory of God and the Transfiguration of Christ* (London: Longmans Green, 1949), p. 81.
12. B.F. Westcott, *The Gospel According to John* (London: John Murray, 1908), new impression, p. 291.
13. Quoted by Ramsey in *Glory of God*, pp. 140–1.
14. *Theological Dictionary*, p. 249.
15. *The Complete English Poems of John Donne*, edited by C.A. Patrides (London: Dent, 1985), pp. 454–6 (p. 455).
16. *Essential Book of Poetry: Five Centuries of Verse* (London: Chancellor Press, 1994), pp. 105–7.
17. *The Crucified God* (London: SCM, 1974), p. 205.
18. *The Glory of the Lord: A Theological Aesthetic* (Edinburgh: T&T Clark, 1989), Vol. VII, p. 211. This is the last of a seven-volume work on the theme of God's glory.
19. Hanson, *Christian Doctrine of God*, p. 15.
20. Kittel, *Theological Dictionary*, p. 249.
21. *Being as Communion*, p. 130.
22. *Against the Heresies*, IV.20.7.

23. Jürgen Moltmann, *The Trinity and the Kingdom of God* (London: SCM, 1980), pp. 113–4.

CHAPTER 6: The Invitation of Christ

1. Herbert J. Ryan, 'Episcopalians, Pentecostalism and The Anglican Tradition', *St Luke's Journal of Theology*, 18 (1975), pp. 123–49 (p. 133).
2. 'Anglican Tradition', p. 133.
3. *Revelations of Divine Love*, chapter 40, quoted by Ryan, p. 134.
4. *The Fire of Love*, quoted by Ryan, pp. 135–6.
5. From 'Rite A' in *The Alternative Service Book 1980*.
6. 'Prayer Before Receiving the Body and Blood of Christ' in *The Prayers and Meditations of St Anselm*, translated by Benedicta Ward (London: Penguin Books, 1973). pp. 100–1.
7. *Ecclesiastical Polity*, v.lxvii.2 (Everyman's Edition II, London: J.M. Dent, 1940), p. 320.
8. 'The Holy Communion', in *George Herbert: The Complete English Poems*, edited by John Tobin (London: Penguin Books, 1991), pp. 46–7.
9. 'Hymns of the Lord's Supper: 54', in J. Ernest Rattenbury, *The Eucharistic Hymns of John and Charles Wesley* (Ohio: OSL Publications, 1990).
10. 'After Communion', in *Signs of Grace: Sacraments in Poetry and Grace*, edited by David Brown and David Fuller (London: Cassell, 1995), p. 60.
11. *Autobiography of a Saint*, translated by Ronald Knox (London: Fount, 1977), pp. 82–3.
12. T.F. Torrance, *Theology in Reconstruction* (London: SCM, 1965), p. 263.
13. For a fuller account see my 'The Cross, Our Worship and Our Living' in *Atonement Today*, edited by Goldingay.
14. 'Lectures on Hebrews' (1518) in *Luther's Works*, Vol. 29 (St Louis: Concordia, 1968), p. 226.
15. See Alan J. Torrance, *Persons in Communion* (Edinburgh: T&T Clark, 1996), pp. 325–55.
16. John Calvin, *Hebrews* (Grand Rapids: Eerdmans, 1853), p. 67.
17. See James B. Torrance, 'The Vicarious Humanity of Christ', in *The Incarnation*, edited by Thomas F. Torrance (Edinburgh: Handsel Press, 1981), pp.127–47; 'The Doctrine of the Trinity in our Con-

temporary Situation', in *The Forgotten Trinity* (London: BCC/CCBI, 1991), Vol. 3, pp. 3–17; and in *Worship, Community and the Triune God of Grace* (Carlisle: Paternoster Press, 1996).

18. I borrow the labels of *task* and *gift* from Thomas A. Smail, *The Giving Gift: The Holy Spirit in Person* (London: Darton, Longman and Todd, 1994), pp. 201–14.

19. *Persons in Communion*, p. 314.

20. *Against Heresies*, 5: Preface.

21. 'Statement on the Eucharist', Anglican-Roman Catholic International Commission, *The Final Report* (London: CTS/SPCK, 1982), para. 6, p. 14.

22. *Promise of Trinitarian Theology*, p. 148.

23. *Promise of Trinitarian Theology*, p. 148.

24. The Doctrine Commission of the Church of England, *The Mystery of Salvation* (London: CHP, 1996), p. 35.

25. 'The Invitation', in *Complete English Poems*, edited by Tobin, pp. 169–70.

26. 'An Epistle Containing the Strange Medical Experience of Karshish, the Arab Physician', in *Robert Browning: Selected Poetry*, edited by Daniel Karlin (London: Penguin Books, 1989), pp. 76–84.

27. P.T. Forsyth, *The Soul of Prayer* (London: Independent Press, 1916), pp. 90–2.

28. For an exception to the rule see the eucharistic prayer of the Third Order of Holy Communion in *A Prayer Book for Australia* (Alexandria: Broughton Books, 1995), pp. 176–7, which allows for the breaking of the bread during the prayer.

29. 'The Holy Communion', in *Complete English Poems*, edited by Tobin, pp. 46–7.

30. For late sixteenth-century and seventeenth-century Anglican, Presbyterian and Independent views of eucharistic consecration see my *Evangelical Eucharistic Thought in the Church of England* (Cambridge: CUP, 1993), pp. 34–6, 42, 47–9.

31. 'The Cross', in *Complete English Poems*, edited by Tobin, pp. 154–5.

32. For a history and analysis of the Sanctus in Jewish and Christian worship see Bryan D. Spinks, *The Sanctus in the Eucharistic Prayer* (Cambridge: CUP, 1991).

33. 'The Banquet', in *Complete English Poems*, edited by Tobin, pp. 170–2.

34. 'Baxter: The Reformation of the Liturgy 1661', in Jasper and Cuming, *Prayers of the Eucharist*, pp. 193–8 (p. 196).

35. 'Love (3)', in *Complete English Poems*, edited by Tobin, p.178.
36. Alasdair Heron, *Table and Tradition* (Edinburgh: Handsel Press, 1983), pp. 24, 32.
37. From his lectures at St John's College, Nottingham in the 1980s.

CHAPTER 7: The Searching of the Spirit

1. *On the thrice holy hymn*, PG 95, 60, quoted by F. X. Durrwell, *Holy Spirit of God* (London: Geoffrey Chapman, 1986), p. 34.
2. See Max Turner, *The Holy Spirit and Spiritual Gifts Then and Now* (Carlisle: Paternoster Press, 1996), pp. 1–3.
3. 'Statement of Faith' in *Nicene and Post Nicene Fathers*, Vol. IV, pp. 84–5 (p. 84).
4. *On the Spirit*, 1.
5. *Fifth Theological Oration*, 26.
6. See Steven J. Land, *Pentecostal Spirituality: A Passion for the Kingdom* (Sheffield: Sheffield Academic Press, 1994), pp.198–9.
7. Quoted by Land in *Pentecostal Spirituality*, p. 17.
8. Michael Welker, *God the Spirit* (Minneapolis: Fortress Press, 1994), p. 233.
9. Traditionally the procession of the Spirit is not related to the begetting of the Son. In eastern theology they are parallel movements. In western theology the begetting of the Son is logically prior to the procession of the Spirit because the Spirit is the mutual love which the Father and Son have for each other. However, in recent years a number of (western) theologians have sought to express a more intrinsic relationship between the Son and Spirit which is closer to the pattern of Jesus' life (where he is born, ministers and is raised by the Father through the Spirit) and to the experience of Christian life (where Christ comes to us in the Spirit). See Durrwell, *Holy Spirit of God*; Moltmann, *Trinity and the Kingdom of God*, e.g. 'The Father utters his eternal Word in the eternal breathing out of his Spirit, pp. 170–1, *The Spirit of Life: A Universal Affirmation* (London: SCM, 1992); Smail, *Giving Gift*; Thomas G. Weinandy, *The Father's Spirit of Sonship* (Edinburgh: T&T Clark, 1995); Edward Yarnold, 'The Trinitarian Implications of Luke and Acts', *The Heythrop Journal*, VII (1966) 18–32. Weinandy's work is an important recent study in which he argues systematically and convincingly that 'the Son is begotten by the Father in the Spirit' (p. 17).

Notes

10. *Giving Gift,* pp. 99–107.
11. See Articles XXV and XXVII. The Thirty-nine Articles can be found in most copies of *The Book of Common Prayer* (1662).
12. *Anglican-Orthodox Dialogue: The Moscow Agreed Statement,* edited by Kallistos Ware and Colin Davey (London: SPCK, 1977), p. 91.
13. This Pentecost hymn is traditionally sung at the ordination of priests and bishops and is often used at confirmations.
14. *Empowering Presence,* p. 806.
15. *Pentecostal Spirituality,* p. 98.
16. For further development of the relationship between the kingdom and the *Abba* address see Jürgen Moltmann, *The Way of Jesus Christ: Christology in Messianic Dimensions* (London, SCM, 1990), pp. 142–5.
17. *Being as Communion,* p. 140.
18. *Against Heresies,* 3.24.1.
19. *Giving Gift,* p. 27. See also pp. 49, 67, 73, 109, 173–4, 193, 206.
20. See John Wesley, *A Plain Account of Christian Perfection* (London: Epworth Press).
21. The line 'Take away the love of sinning' appears in some versions of Charles Wesley's hymn *Love Divine, all loves excelling,* see *Songs and Hymns of Fellowship* and *Mission Praise.* In fact the original line which appeared in *Hymns For Those That Seek And Those That Have Redemption In The Blood of Christ,* 1747, was 'Take away our power of sinning'. In 1757 Fletcher of Madeley expressed objections to the line on the grounds that it effectively asked God to remove our capacity for moral choice. He suggested alternatives such as 'Take away our bent towards sinning'. The whole verse in which it appears was omitted by John Wesley when he published *A Collection of Hymns For The Use Of The People Called Methodists* in 1780. However, Primitive Methodists, American Methodists, Bible Christians, Baptists and others retained its usage in an adapted form and so bequeathed its use to some modern hymnals. I am grateful to my former colleague David Frudd for information on the history of the line.

CHAPTER 8: The Trinity, Worship and Mission

1. P.T. Forsyth, *Missions in State and Church: Sermons and Addresses* (London: Hodder and Stoughton, 1908), pp. 270–1.
2. The Lambeth Conference, 1988, *The Truth Shall Make You Free* (London: CHP, 1988), p. 28.

3. 'On Psalm 118', *Luther's Works*, edited by Jaroslav Pelikan and Daniel Poellot, Vol. 14 (St Louis: Concordia Publishing House), p. 81.
4. On the issue of the mutuality between God and the world see Hardy, *God's Ways with the World*. On the question of God's expansive nature and particularly its relationship with our worship see the highly illuminating section in Appendix A of Daniel W. Hardy and David F. Ford, *Jubilate: Theology in Praise* (London: Darton, Longman and Todd, 1984), pp. 161–2.
5. From 'La Corona' in Patrides, *English Poems*, p. 430.
6. 'The Sanctus', from 'Rite A' in *The Alternative Service Book 1980*.

Recommended Reading

Bauckham, Richard, *The Theology of the Book of Revelation* (Cambridge: CUP, 1993)

Byrne, James B. (ed.), *The Christian Understanding of God Today* (Dublin: The Columba Press, 1993)

Doctrine Commission of the Church of England, *We Believe in the Holy Spirit* (London: BCC, 1989)

Gunton, Colin E., *The One, the Three and the Many: God, Creation and the Culture of Modernity* (Cambridge: CUP, 1993)

Heron, Alasdair I.C. (ed.), *The Forgotten Trinity: 3 A Selection of Papers* (London: BCC/CCBI, 1991)

Kasper, Walter, *The God of Jesus Christ* (London: SCM, 1984)

Moltmann, Jürgen, *The Trinity and the Kingdom of God: The Doctrine of God* (London: SCM, 1980)

Smail, Thomas A., *The Giving Gift: The Holy Spirit in Person* (London: Darton, Longman and Todd, 1994).

The Forgotten Trinity: 1 The Report of the BCC Study Commission on Trinitarian Doctrine Today (London: BCC, 1989)

Thompson, John, *Modern Trinitarian Perspectives* (Oxford: OUP, 1994)

Torrance, James B., *Worship, Community and the Triune God of Grace* (Carlisle: Paternoster Press, 1996)

Torrance, Thomas F., *The Christian Doctrine of God: One Being in Three Persons* (Edinburgh: T&T Clark, 1996)

Weinandy, Thomas G., *The Father's Gift of Sonship* (Edinburgh: T&T Clark, 1995)

NAME AND SUBJECT INDEX

ooooooooo

The subject indexing is necessarily selective and generally omits theological terms referred to pervasively in the text.

Name and Subject Index

INDEX OF BIBLICAL REFERENCES

ooooooooo

241

Index of Biblical References